S0-CLG-644

D1525982

america's economy

1989 annual

David L. Bender, *Publisher*
Bruno Leone, *Executive Editor*
Bonnie Szumski, *Senior Editor*
Janelle Rohr, *Senior Editor*
Susan Bursell, *Editor*
William Dudley, *Editor*
Robert Anderson, *Assistant Editor*
Karin Swisher, *Assistant Editor*
Lisa Orr, *Assistant Editor*
Diana Shellenberger, *Assistant Editor*

Theodore Lownik Library
Illinois Benedictine College
Lisle, Illinois 60532

greenhaven press, inc.

PO Box 289009
San Diego, CA 92128-9009

338.973
A512
suppl.
1989

© 1989 by Greenhaven Press, Inc.

ISBN 0-89908-550-4
ISSN 0889-4299

contents

Editor's Note   ***Opposing Viewpoints SOURCES*** provide a wealth of opinions on important issues of the day. The annual supplements focus on the topics that continue to generate debate. Readers will find that *Opposing Viewpoints SOURCES* become exciting barometers of today's controversies. This is achieved in three ways. First, by expanding previous chapter topics. Second, by adding new materials which are timeless in nature. And third, by adding recent topical issues not dealt with in previous volumes or annuals.

Viewpoints

"[The] list of questions that should be considered in thinking about budget policy . . . is formidable."

The Budget Deficit: An Overview

Herbert Stein

I would like to identify a number of issues that are relevant to budget policy and that could be discussed objectively. . . . It is not my intention to give answers to the questions I raise here. . . .

How Does the Budget Deficit Matter?

There are three views of this question:

• The budget deficit may be regarded as a disequilibrium that cannot go on forever, the ending of which will precipitate a crisis of some sort. One conception of this unsustainable situation is that the government debt rises without limit as a proportion of gross national product (GNP). Then the interest burden becomes intolerable or the debt becomes unsalable, and the government resorts to inflation as its only escape. In the recent American situation attention has been focused on another aspect of unsustainability. Some hold that the continuing budget deficit causes continuing trade deficits financed by foreign acquisition of dollars. Foreigners will not want to go on acquiring dollars forever. When they stop, the dollar will decline, creating difficulties for the American economy. Although the end of either of these processes—government debt accumulation or dollar liability accumulation—may be a long way off, markets may anticipate that time and cause an increase of interest rates or decline of the dollar much sooner. Moreover, the reaction will not come gradually but suddenly, as a response to some event—like an election—that will be interpreted as significantly changing the outlook.

The Disequilibrium Aspect

• A second view belittles the disequilibrium aspect of the deficit. It maintains that in fact deficits of the now foreseeable size would not raise the ratio of debt to GNP, and even somewhat larger deficits

would raise that ratio slowly and still leave it below levels we have lived with easily in the postwar period. The accumulation of dollars in foreign hands could go on for a very long time, if not indefinitely, as long as the United States remains a favorable environment for investment. The real problem is that deficits of the recent and prospective size, even if they can go on indefinitely, have an adverse economic effect. They absorb some of the nation's private saving into financing consumption (government spending) and keep it from being used to finance investment. This reduces the long-run rate of economic growth.

• A third view rejects both the disequilibrium and the growth-retarding arguments and sees the deficit as another kind of tax. When the government borrows, it takes on obligations for interest payments that will have to be paid out of taxes in the future. That is, it incurs liabilities for current taxpayers—liabilities that will be assessed later on some future tax base. Taxpayers, seeing that this liability is being incurred, will save to have the future income that will enable them to pay the future taxes. This saving will offset the absorption of saving in the government deficit, so that the amount of saving available for private investment is not reduced by the deficit. The "deficit tax" will have a different effect from other taxes in the same way that a cigarette tax, for example, has a different effect from an income tax; and it will have only that kind of difference.

How Much Does a Deficit Affect Growth?

If we accept the idea that the main effect of deficits is the reduction of the growth rate, we still have to ask how big the effect is. Merely to say that deficits retard growth does not tell us by how much the deficit should be reduced or that it should be reduced at all. Reducing the deficit to increase investment has its costs—most generally it requires cutting consumption, private or public. The gain in

Herbert Stein, "Now, Please, Can We Begin To Discuss the Budget?" *The AEI Economist*, December 1988. Reprinted with permission from The American Enterprise Institute for Public Policy Research.

growth from reducing the deficit has to be compared with the costs of doing so, and that requires an estimate of the size of the gain.

Opinions of economists about how much growth would increase as a result of reducing the deficit by, say, 1 percent of GNP, differ significantly. The answer depends on how much of the growth of output per worker or per hour of work comes from the increase in the net capital stock, which is presumably affected by the size of the deficit. (This abstracts, for the present, from the possible effects on growth of the means by which the deficit is reduced.) Some economists see the growth in output per worker as almost entirely dependent on the growth of the capital stock, which brings with it the incorporation of new technology into production as well as the sheer increase in the quantity of capital. Other economists attribute a much smaller share of the growth of output per worker to the increase in the capital stock, emphasizing the improvement of technology that is incorporated in the replacement of the existing capital stock, the increased quality of the labor force, improvements in economic organization, and gains from the increase in the scale of production.

The following indicates, crudely, the significance of the differing estimates on this point. Suppose that with the existing size of the deficit, as a fraction of GNP, output per worker would rise by 2 percent per year. On a high estimate of the contribution of capital, reducing the deficit by 1 percent of GNP would raise the growth rate to 2.25 percent per year. On a low estimate the growth rate might be 2.0833. If continued the 1 percent reduction in the deficit would make the per worker GNP about 5 percent higher at the end of twenty years on the higher estimate of the effect of investment. On the lower estimate the gain in per worker GNP at the end of twenty years would be about 1.5 percent.

An Explicit Assumption

The size of these growth gains from a lower deficit would depend on how the deficit reduction is brought about. If the deficit is reduced by cutting government expenditures on education, research, or productive government infrastructure, like roads, there may be little contribution to growth. Similarly, if the deficit is reduced by raising taxes that inhibit saving or impair economic efficiency, the contribution to growth will be limited, depending on the magnitude of the adverse effect of the taxes. The question of the economic effect of taxation will come up in the discussion below.

In any case, a rational decision about the appropriate size of the deficit or surplus, from the standpoint of the rate of economic growth, will depend on an estimate or assumption about the magnitude of these effects. And however uncertain the estimates of this magnitude are, it is better to

make the assumption explicit than to leave it implicit, where it may be entirely outside the range of reasonable estimates.

Is the Rate of Growth the Government's Business?

Some argue on the one hand that the rate of economic growth is not a matter that the government should be concerned with and that it should not make decisions about the budget and surplus with the intention of influencing the rate of growth. They say that individuals can express their interest in their future incomes and those of their descendants by their actions, principally by saving. If individuals are dissatisfied with the future growth they can expect, given the government's deficit and other policies, they can manage their own affairs to compensate.

"Opinions of economists about how much growth would increase as a result of reducing the deficit . . . differ significantly."

On the other hand, others believe that citizens do have a legitimate concern with the growth of the national economy distinct from their concern with their own future incomes. In part while this is a concern with future national security and ability to bear military burdens, it may also be a concern with the value of living in a society where visible growth is to be expected, a mood generating optimism and social solidarity. Others may express a social concern with growth that runs in the opposite direction, holding that there is a social interest in restricting the rate of growth because growth has negative environmental effects and also possibly negative cultural and moral effects. (This was the point of the zero growth movement that was popular about twenty years ago but has faded since the actual growth rate has declined.) Without regard to the direction of the connection between growth and social values, in this view national growth is as legitimate an object of government concern as the health of the population or even the education of the population.

An Intermediate View

An intermediate view is that the government cannot help affecting the rate of growth, by its tax policy, investment in public infrastructure, and education policy as well as by its deficit or surplus. The government should be concerned with what it is doing. One application of this view is that the government should try to manage the totality of its effects on growth or, more narrowly, on the stock of capital, so that the net result is the same as if there were no government.

How Much Do We Care about Growth?

Suppose we have decided that deficits and surpluses affect growth and have formed an opinion about how big this effect is per amount of deficit or surplus and have decided that the rate of growth is a legitimate concern of government; the question still remains how much we do or should care, because that is essential for deciding what we are willing to sacrifice for growth. This is a question to which there is no objective answer. People will think what they think about it, just as in their individual capacities people have different attitudes toward providing for their own future and their children's. Some might say that providing for future growth is not very important, because America is already very rich and will probably become richer still without any special effort of government in that direction. Others might say that we have an obligation to make our children as much richer as we are richer than our parents were. Of particular relevance to the present generation is the prospect that in the next generation the percentage of the population that is retired and that the society has assumed an obligation to support will be much larger than it is now, which must constitute a special case for trying to build up the national income by accumulating capital in advance of that time.

Would Raising Taxes Choke Off the Expansion?

A prominent idea in current discussion is that taxes must not be raised because that would endanger continuation of the economic expansion. Implicit in this idea is the belief that the reduction of taxes in 1981 was a major cause of the long economic expansion that began in 1982.

Two Arguments

The alleged connection between raising taxes and the expansion comes in two forms—demand side, or Keynesian, and supply side. The demand-side argument is that an increase in taxes reduces the after-tax income that private parties have available to spend, reduces total expenditure for the purchase of goods and services, and so reduces total output of goods and services and total employment. The counter to this argument is that an increase in taxes would be matched by some combination of increased government expenditures and reduced federal borrowing that would offset the negative effect of the tax increase on demand. A weaker and more plausible version of the demand-side argument is that a large tax increase taking effect within a short period might depress demand and output because the offsets would not come into force simultaneously. But how big this tax increase would have to be to cause this disturbance is a matter of conjecture.

If the demand-side argument is valid, a reduction of the deficit brought about by the increase of revenue resulting from economic growth or by restraint of government expenditures would have the same depressing effect as a reduction of the deficit brought about by raising taxes.

"The alleged connection between raising taxes and the [economic] expansion comes in two forms—demand side, or Keynesian, and supply side."

The supply-side argument is that increased taxes would endanger continuation of the economic expansion by reducing incentives to supply labor and capital to the productive process. Although the magnitude of these incentive effects is a matter of considerable disagreement, the principal counter to the supply-side argument insofar as it is applied to the continuation of the expansion is a matter of timing. The tax effects on saving and labor supply are likely to come slowly, because these effects depend on changes of life styles that do not respond quickly to changes in economic incentives. . . .

Can Raising the Revenue Reduce the Deficit?

This is the Parkinson's Law question, referring to an English political scientist who propounded the "law" that government expenditures rise to equal the revenue. Since expenditures in the United States have now risen to exceed the revenue substantially, the law probably needs to be restated. We would probably have to say now that the government will generate a certain size or path of the deficit and that an increase in the revenue will alter not the deficit but only the expenditures. This leaves open the question of how that certain size or path of the deficit is arrived at, since it has changed substantially in our lifetime. It also implies that this deficit cannot be affected by increases of revenue that come with growth of the economy any more than it can be affected by increases of revenue that result from tax increases. In other words, Parkinson's Law casts doubt on the popular idea of growing our way out of the deficit. Parkinson's Law also casts doubt on the possibility of reducing the deficit by cutting expenditures, since it implies that the idea of the proper size of deficits is fixed at any moment and governs all other decisions, so that if expenditures are cut taxes will be cut also.

Some recent study of Parkinson's Law leaves the issue in doubt. Our main experience with tax increases has been in wartime. In general, the end of wars has been accompanied by reduction of the wartime deficits, reduction of the wartime taxes, and some increase in expenditures above their prewar levels. That crude evidence suggests that some part of revenue increases resulting from tax increases is spent but not all. More sophisticated econometric analysis is inconclusive.

The Parkinson's Law question has been given an unusually precise significance today by another law, Gramm-Rudman-Hollings, which mandates a certain path for the reduction of the deficit. Several views of the relation between the two laws are possible:

• The Gramm-Rudman-Hollings deficit reduction path will be followed, whether or not taxes are raised. The consequence of raising taxes would be more spending but not a smaller deficit than required by Gramm-Rudman-Hollings.

• The Gramm-Rudman-Hollings path will not be followed unless taxes are raised. If taxes are raised, expenditures may be higher than if they were not raised, but that is not the only possibility. Expenditures might be lower because the political defenders of some expenditure programs may be more willing to make concessions as part of a package that includes tax increases.

• The Gramm-Rudman-Hollings path will not be followed in any case, and the deficit will be no smaller if taxes are raised than if they are not.

• The Gramm-Rudman-Hollings path will not be followed, but the deficit will be smaller if taxes are raised than if they are not.

There is no law, neither Parkinson's nor Gramm-Rudman-Hollings, that answers such questions. The answer probably depends on the political and economic situation of the time.

Can Anything Be Said about Expenditures in General?

Some discussion of the budget implies that expenditures are too high, without regard to the specific object of the expenditures, and that any cut of expenditures, whatever the specific object, is a good thing. This is an important point, because if it is not accepted, the common argument that the deficit must be reduced, but only by reducing expenditures, and that the deficit is caused by excessive expenditures, becomes inadequate. It then becomes necessary to argue about the merit of particular expenditures, which makes the whole issue much more difficult than it otherwise seems.

Two Propositions

The case for saying that expenditures in general are too high seems to rest on two propositions. One is that government expenditures constitute an infringement on the freedom of private parties to use their own income and may pave the way for the infringement of other freedoms as well. The other is that government expenditures are inherently excessive and wasteful because they are made or influenced by people who are not spending their own money. Each of these arguments is open to two qualifications. In the first place they are clearly not equally applicable to all kinds of expenditures, which raises the problem of choosing which to cut and even raises the possibility that the complaint is

inconsequential for some expenditures relative to the benefit from the expenditure. Second, the arguments seem to have been as applicable to the federal budget of Calvin Coolidge, 3 percent of GNP, as to the budget of Ronald Reagan, 22 percent of GNP. Indeed, the arguments seem to run against having any government at all. If we believe, however, that some expenditures are worthwhile despite their impairment of freedom and their wastefulness, we get back to the practical and difficult question of whether we have now gone too far.

"Some discussion of the budget implies that expenditures are too high, without regard to the specific object of the expenditures."

If a compelling case cannot be made against expenditures in general, rational budgeting would have to consider the effects of the different kinds of expenditures included in the budget. I am not going to list the questions that would be raised in such an effort: they are diverse and mainly obvious. I would suggest at this point only that we are as far from an informed, constructive discussion of expenditures as we are from one of deficits and taxes.

Is Rational Budgeting Possible?

This list of questions that should be considered in thinking about budget policy, itself far from complete, is formidable. It suggests that rational budgeting—that is, budgeting based on good information about the relations between means and ends and explicit weighing of ends—is impossible. But since budget decisions have to be made, this line of thinking leads to the advocacy of rules that are admittedly arbitrary but allegedly superior to the flawed results of attempted rationality. Such rules include the balanced-budget rule, the expenditure-ceiling rule, the Gramm-Rudman rules for dividing up expenditure cuts and other proposals for freezes or across-the-board cuts, and the "no new taxes" rule.

This issue, however, whether the attempt to achieve rationality is worthwhile and superior to feasible alternatives, itself deserves more explicit discussion than it has so far received by government decision makers. . . .

Although I have no illusions about the possibility of giving firm and objective answers to the questions raised here, there can be no doubt that they are relevant.

Herbert Stein is a senior fellow of the American Enterprise Institute, a public policy research organization.

"Large and persistent deficits are slowly but inexorably damaging the economy."

viewpoint 2

Budget Deficits Threaten the Economy

Alan Greenspan

It is beguiling to contemplate the strong economy of recent years in the context of very large deficits and to conclude that the concerns about the adverse effects of the deficit on the economy have been misplaced. But this argument is fanciful. The deficit already has begun to eat away at the foundations of our economic strength. And the need to deal with it is becoming ever more urgent. To the extent that some of the negative effects of deficits have not as yet been felt, they have been merely postponed, not avoided. Moreover, the scope for further such avoidance is shrinking.

Muted Effects

To some degree, the effects of the federal budget deficits over the past several years have been muted by two circumstances, both of which are currently changing rapidly. One was the rather large degree of slack in the economy in the early years of the current expansion. This slack meant that the economy could accommodate growing demands from both the private and public sectors. In addition, to the extent that these demands could not be accommodated from U.S. resources, we went abroad and imported them. This can be seen in our large trade and current account deficits. By now, however, the slack in the U.S. economy has contracted substantially. And, it has become increasingly clear that reliance on foreign sources of funds is not possible or desirable over extended periods. As these sources are reduced along with our trade deficit, other sources must be found, or demands for saving curtailed. The choices are limited; as will become clear, the best option for the American people is a further reduction in the federal budget deficit, and the need for such reduction is becoming more pressing.

Alan Greenspan, statement to the National Economic Commission in Washington, DC, November 16, 1988.

Owing to significant efforts by the administration and the Congress, coupled with strong economic growth, the deficit has shrunk from 5 to 6 percent of gross national product a few years ago to about 3 percent of GNP today. Such a deficit, nevertheless, is still very large by historical standards. Since World War II, the actual budget deficit has exceeded 3 percent of GNP only in the 1975 recession period and in the recent deficit experience beginning in 1982. On a cyclically adjusted or structural basis, the deficit has exceeded 3 percent of potential GNP only in the period since 1983.

Government deficits, however, place pressure on resources and credit markets, only if they are not offset by saving elsewhere in the economy. If the pool of private saving is small, federal deficits and private investment will be in keen competition for funds, and private investment will lose.

Low Private Saving

The United States deficits of recent years are threatening precisely because they have been occurring in the context of private saving that is low by both historical and international standards. Historically, net personal plus business saving in the United States in the 1980s is about 3 percentage points lower relative to GNP than its average in the preceding three decades. Internationally, government deficits have been quite common among the major industrial countries in the 1980s, but private saving rates in most of these countries have exceeded the deficits by very comfortable margins. In Japan, for example, less than 20 percent of its private saving has been absorbed by government deficits, even though the Japanese general government has been borrowing almost 3 percent of its gross domestic product in the 1980s. In contrast, over half of private U.S. saving in the 1980s has been absorbed by the combined deficits of the federal and state and local sectors.

Under these circumstances, such large and persistent deficits are slowly but inexorably damaging the economy. The damage occurs because deficits tend to pull resources away from net private investment. And a reduction in net investment has reduced the rate of growth of the nation's capital stock. This in turn has meant less capital per worker than would otherwise have been the case, and this will surely engender a shortfall in labor productivity growth and, with it, a shortfall in growth of the standard of living.

The process by which government deficits divert resources from net private investment is part of the broader process of redirecting the allocation of real resources that inevitably accompanies the activities of the federal government. The federal government can preempt resources from the private sector or direct their usage by a number of different means, the most important of which are: 1) deficit spending, on- or off-budget; 2) tax financed spending; 3) regulation mandating private activities such as pollution control or safety equipment installation, which are financed by industry through the issuance of debt instruments; and 4) government guarantees of private borrowing.

Not Interest Sensitive

What deficit spending and regulatory measures have in common is that the extent to which resources are preempted by government actions, directly or indirectly, is not sensitive to the rate of interest. The federal government, for example, will finance its budget deficit in full, irrespective of the interest rate it must pay to raise the funds. Similarly, a government-mandated private activity will almost always be financed irrespective of the interest rate that exists. Borrowing with government-guaranteed debt may be only partly interest sensitive, but the guarantees have the effect of preempting resources from those without access to riskless credit. Government spending fully financed by taxation does, of course, preempt real resources from the private sector, but the process works through channels other than real interest rates.

"The federal government . . . will finance its budget deficit in full, irrespective of the interest rate it must pay to raise the funds."

Purely private activities, on the other hand, are, to a greater or lesser extent, responsive to interest rates. The demand for mortgages, for example, falls off dramatically as mortgage interest rates rise. Inventory demand is, clearly, a function of short-term interest rates, and the level of interest rates, as they are reflected in the cost of capital, is a key element in the decision on whether to expand or modernize productive capacity. Hence, to the extent that there are more resources demanded in an economy than are available to be financed, interest rates will rise until sufficient excess demand is finally crowded out. The crowded out demand cannot, of course, be that of the federal government, directly or indirectly, since government demand does not respond to rising interest rates. Rather, real interest rates will rise to the point that private borrowing is reduced sufficiently to allow the entire requirements of the federal on- and off-budget deficit, and all its collateral guarantees and mandated activities, to be met.

No Alternative

In real terms, there is no alternative to a diversion of real resources from the private to the public sector. In the short run, interest rates can be held down if the Federal Reserve accommodates the excess demand for funds through a more expansionary monetary policy. But this will only engender an acceleration of inflation and, ultimately, will have little if any effect on the allocation of real resources between the private and public sectors.

The Treasury has been a large and growing customer in financial markets in recent years. It has acquired, on average, roughly 25 percent of the total funds borrowed in domestic credit markets over the last four years [since 1984], up from less than 15 percent in the 1970s. For the Treasury to raise its share of total credit flows in this fashion, it must push other borrowers aside.

The more interest responsive are the total demands of these other, private borrowers—the less will the equilibrium interest rate be pushed up by the increase in Treasury borrowing. That is, the greater the decline in the quantity of funds demanded, and the associated spending to be financed, for a given rise in interest rates, the lower will be the rate. In contrast, if private borrowing and spending are resistant, interest rates will have to rise more before enough private spending gives way. In either case, private investment is crowded out by higher real interest rates.

Even if private investment were not as interest elastic as it appears to be, crowding out of private spending by the budget deficit would occur dollar-for-dollar if the total supply of saving were fixed. To the extent that the supply of saving is induced to increase, both the equilibrium rise in interest rates and the amount of crowding out will be less. However, even if more saving can be induced in the short run, it will be permanently lowered in the long run to the extent that real income growth is curtailed by reduced capital formation.

But aggregate investment is only part of the process through which the structure of production is affected by high real interest rates. Higher real interest rates also induce both consumers and businesses to concentrate their purchases disproportionately on immediately consumable goods and, of course, services. When real interest rates are high, purchasers and producers of long-lived assets such as real estate and capital equipment pull back. They cannot afford the debt carrying costs at high interest rates, or if financed with available cash, the forgone interest income resulting from this expenditure of the cash. Under such conditions, one would expect the GNP to be disproportionately composed of short-lived goods—food, clothing, services, etc.

Indeed, statistical analysis demonstrates such a relationship—that is, a recent decline in the average service life of all consumption and investment goods and a systematic tendency for this average to move inversely with real rates of interest. That is, the higher real interest rates, the heavier the concentration on short-lived assets. Parenthetically, the resulting shift toward shorter-lived investment goods means that more *gross* investment is required to provide for replacement of the existing capital stock as well as for the *net* investment necessary to raise tomorrow's living standards. Thus, the current relatively high ratio of gross investment to GNP in this country is a deceptive indicator of the additions to our capital stock.

"The presumption that the deficit is benign is clearly false."

Not surprisingly, we have already experienced a disturbing decline in the level of net investment as a share of GNP. Net investment has fallen to 4.7 percent of GNP in the 1980s from an average level of 6.7 percent in the 1970s and even higher in the 1960s. Moreover, it is low, not only by our own historical standards, but by international standards as well.

International comparisons of net investment should be viewed with some caution because of differences in the measurement of depreciation and in other technical details. Nevertheless, the existing data do indicate that total net private and public investment as a share of gross domestic product over the period between 1980 and 1986 was lower in the United States than in any of the other major industrial countries except the United Kingdom.

It is important to recognize as I indicated earlier that the negative effects of federal deficits on growth in the capital stock may be attenuated for a while by several forces in the private sector. One is a significant period of output growth in excess of potential GNP growth—such as occurred over much of the past six years [since 1982]—which undoubtedly boosts sales and profit expectations and, hence, business investment. Such rates of output growth, of course, cannot persist, making this factor inherently temporary in nature.

Another factor tending to limit the decline in investment spending would be any tendency for saving to respond positively to the higher interest rates that deficits would bring. The supply of domestic private saving has some interest elasticity, as people put off spending when borrowing costs are high and returns from their financial assets are favorable. But most analysts find that this elasticity is not sufficiently large to matter much.

An Important Addition

Finally, net inflows of foreign saving can be, as recent years have demonstrated, an important addition to saving. In the 1980s, foreign saving has kept the decline in the gross investment-GNP ratio, on average, to only moderate dimensions (slightly more than one-half percentage point) compared with the 1970s, while the federal deficit rose by about 2½ percentage points relative to GNP. Net inflows of foreign saving have amounted, on average, to almost 2 percent of GNP, an unprecedented level.

Opinions differ about the relative importance of high United States interest rates, changes in the after-tax return to investment in the United States, and changes in perception of the relative risks of investment in various countries and currencies in bringing about the foreign capital inflow. Whatever its source, had we not experienced this addition to our saving, our interest rates would have been even higher and domestic investment lower. Indeed, since 1985, when the appetite of private investors for dollar assets seems to have waned, the downtrend in real long-term rates has become erratic, tending to stall with the level still historically high.

Looking ahead, the continuation of foreign saving at current levels is questionable. Evidence for the United States and for most other major industrial nations over the last 100 years indicates that such sizable foreign net capital inflows have not persisted and, hence, may not be a reliable substitute for domestic saving on a long-term basis. In other words, domestic investment tends to be supported by domestic saving alone in the long run.

Let me conclude by reiterating my central message. The presumption that the deficit is benign is clearly false. It is partly responsible for the decline in the net investment ratio in the 1980s to a sub-optimal level. Allowing it to go on courts a dangerous corrosion of our economy. Fortunately, we have it in our power to reverse this process, thereby avoiding potentially significant reductions in our standard of living.

Alan Greenspan is chairman of the Federal Reserve System.

"Placing the blame for the serious and stubborn problems facing the U.S. economy... on budget deficits doesn't hold up."

viewpoint 3

Budget Deficits Do Not Threaten the Economy

Peter L. Bernstein

Good theory should be applicable just about everywhere. The second law of thermodynamics respects no national borders. Nor do the law of supply and demand, the Fisher effect relating interest rates to inflation, and the positive relationship between risk and return.

We know that these theoretical economic concepts do not always work out perfectly in the real world. On the other hand, we know that they are essential if we are to understand and explain prices, interest rates and investment decisions. These concepts have worked about as well in Santiago and Sydney as they have worked in Tokyo and San Francisco.

Seen from this standpoint, the broad acceptance of the current theory that budget deficits threaten the national economy—indeed, that they must be the first order of business for President Bush—is all the more puzzling. This theory is inconsistent across national borders.

The consensus view holds that budget deficits absorb savings and encourage consumption. The resulting shortage of savings available for private investment pushes real interest rates upward, attracting foreign capital and raising the exchange rate. The rise in the exchange rate sucks in imports and depresses exports, crowding out private investment in the process.

Therefore, we must reduce the budget deficit in order to restrain consumption, increase our domestic saving rate, and reduce our dependence on foreign capital and foreign goods. If we fail to do this, the dollar will fall in the foreign exchange markets and that will be inflationary.

Or so it is believed. But the consequences of fiscal restraint and fiscal profligacy are indeterminate and uncertain.

Peter L. Bernstein, "All the Things Deficits Really Don't Do," *The Wall Street Journal*, November 10, 1988. Reprinted with permission of The Wall Street Journal © 1989 Dow Jones & Company, Inc. All rights reserved.

According to the most popular set of generalizations about the deficit, however, we should expect deficits to correlate positively with interest rates—probably nominal but surely real—and to correlate negatively with the trade balance and with the saving rate.

1. General Gov't. Debt/GDP (in percent)

	1980	1986	RANK
Canada	11.6%	33.7%	1
France	9.1	18.2	2
Italy	61.8	99.2	3
Germany	14.4	22.1	4
Japan	17.3	26.3	5
U.S.	19.8	28.7	6
U.K.	48.1	46.5	7

Source: National Bureau of Economic Research paper derived from OECD data. Following tables are from IMF Financial Statistics Yearbook 1988.

Consider first Table 1, showing the ratio of general government net debt to gross domestic product for the seven major industrial nations from 1980 to 1986. The seven are ranked in order of the rise in their debt/GDP ratios. I have used the percentage change in the ratios here, rather than the absolute change, as the group started with such huge differences among their 1980 levels. (Absolute change is used for rankings in the other tables, where negative percentages are otherwise problematic. But this doesn't assist my argument.)

Two Noteworthy Features

The more rapid the rise in the volume of government debt outstanding between 1980 and 1986, the larger the deficits must have been. Thus, we see that Canada ranked no. 1 with the ratio that rose the most, while Britain landed at the bottom of the list with an actual decline in the ratio of government debt to GDP.

From the viewpoint of an American, two features of this table are noteworthy.

First, the U.S. is far from being the worst sinner in running budget deficits. In fact, the U.S. shows the second-best performance here. Those outstanding examples of economic rectitude, the Germans and the Japanese, had ratios that rose even more than ours, even if by only a small amount.

Second, the level of the U.S. ratio is by no means an outlier. We are in the same ballpark as Japan and Canada. Germany is not so far below us. The U.K. and Italy are far above our level.

The remaining tables, covering interest rates, inflation, the trade balance and the saving ratio, rank the countries in the same manner, with the worst performance ranked no. 1 and the best performance ranked no. 7. In addition, each table includes the Spearman rank coefficient, relating the ranking in that table to the ranking in Table 1. If each of the other variables changed in the same order as the government debt/GDP ratio—which is what the accepted doctrine asserts would be the case—this coefficient would be equal to 1.00.

2. Government Bond Yield (in percent)			
	1980	1986	RANK
Canada	12.5%	9.5%	2
France	13.0	8.4	6
Italy	16.1	10.5	7
Germany	8.5	5.9	1
Japan	9.2	4.9	5
U.S.	11.5	7.7	3
U.K.	13.8	9.9	4
SPEARMAN COEFFICIENT			−0.07

Table 2 shows nominal government bond yields. All seven countries enjoyed declining interest rates for 1980-86. Deficit theory hypothesizes that interest rates should have declined the least where the growth in debt was biggest and should have declined the most where fiscal prudence was adhered to. But we see essentially no relationship in the Spearman coefficient.

No Clear Relationship

Table 3 shows the rates of change in the consumer price index, with Germany having the smallest absolute drop in the inflation rate and ranking no. 1, while Italy, with the biggest drop, ranked no. 7.

The correlation between the change in the inflation rate and the growth in government debt is far from perfect, but it is positive. On the other hand, we can see that there is no clear relationship between budget deficits and changes in the rate of inflation. (Indeed, if we establish the rankings in terms of the percentage change in the inflation rates, the correlation turns out to be a strong negative at −0.62.)

The important feature of Table 3 is in its firm empirical support for the Fisher effect I mentioned at the outset. The correlation between the absolute change in nominal interest rates and the absolute change in inflation is an impressive 0.64.

3. CPI Inflation (in percent)			
	1980	1986	RANK
Canada	10.2%	4.2%	2
France	13.3	2.5	5
Italy	21.3	5.9	7
Germany	5.4	−0.2	1
Japan	7.7	0.6	3
U.S.	11.9	1.9	4
U.K.	18.0	3.4	6
SPEARMAN COEFFICIENT			+0.21

We now come to a crucial point in the argument.

If we deduct inflation rates from nominal interest rates, the difference is equal to what is known as the real interest rate. This is the variable that government borrowing is supposed to push upward, because deficits "absorb" savings, causing trouble for the economy. Therefore, Table 4 shows the levels and changes in real interest rates, calculated by deducting the inflation numbers in Table 3 from the nominal interest rate numbers in Table 2.

4. Real Interest Rates (in percent)			
	1980	1986	RANK
Canada	2.3%	5.3%	7
France	−0.3	5.9	3
Italy	−5.2	4.6	2
Germany	3.1	6.1	5
Japan	1.5	4.3	6
U.S.	−0.4	5.8	4
U.K.	−4.2	6.5	1
SPEARMAN COEFFICIENT			−0.43

The story here is a dramatic one: the correlation is negative, and significantly so. Indeed, the U.K., with the best fiscal performance, had the widest upward movement in real interest rates, while the increase in Canadian interest rates was the smallest despite Canada's ranking at the top of Table 1. The other six countries show only a slight positive correlation.

This result flies in the face of the central element in the accepted doctrine of budget deficits. It should, however, come as no surprise to careful students of this area of economics. Rudolph Penner, senior fellow at the Urban Institute and former chief economist of the Congressional Budget Office, put it this way in the October 1988 issue of *Business Economics*:

"In both Keynesian and classical analysis, one would expect a positive relationship between the deficit and real interest rates. This relationship has been devilishly difficult to document statistically. Although a majority of studies show a positive relationship, often it is not statistically significant, and some studies show a statistically significant negative relationship. More disturbing, small changes in the specification of the models used can change the relationship from positive to negative and vice versa."

5. Trade Balance/GNP (in percent)			
	1980	1986	RANK
Canada	2.09%	1.26%	3
France	−1.23	1.03	4
Italy	−4.81	0.47	6
Germany	−0.21	5.75	7
Japan	0.00	5.20	5
U.S.	−0.57	−4.37	1
U.K.	2.21	−0.76	2
SPEARMAN COEFFICIENT			−0.35

What about the foreign trade balance?

Table 5 shows the ratio of the trade balance—positive for net exports and negative for net imports—as a ratio of GNP [gross national product]. The biggest deterioration puts the U.S. as no. 1, with Germany as no. 7, the "best" foreign trade performance.

Lo and behold—the correlation coefficient is negative once more. The U.S. and the U.K., whose debt/GDP ratio rose the least, show up here with the "worst" foreign-trade performance; they are the only two countries that swung from an export surplus in 1980 to an import surplus in 1986. Italy, with rapid growth in government borrowing and by far the highest level of debt to GDP, ended up with an impressive improvement in its trade balance.

Clearly, many forces other than fiscal policy determine what happens to the foreign trade balance.

The Saving Rate

Well, maybe the saving rate will save the theory.

Table 6 shows the ratio of consumption to GDP. The International Monetary Fund's tabulation is especially useful for our purposes, because the ratio shown here includes government consumption—as opposed to government investment in capital goods—as well as private consumption.

Perhaps the deficit theory finds a fragment of support here—the U.S. had the largest relative rise in consumption among the seven countries. Oh—but we had one of the smallest relative increases in our national debt, so this can have little or nothing to do with U.S. fiscal policy. The relationship between deficits and saving rates appears to be essentially random (although ranking based on percentage rather than absolute changes in saving rates again produces a strong negative Spearman coefficient).

This table makes an important point, but it does not support the accepted theory of deficits. Table 6 tells us loud and clear that high-consumption countries in 1980 tended to be even higher-consumption countries in 1986, and vice versa.

6. Consumption/GDP* (in percent)			
	1980	1986	RANK
Canada	76.7%	81.1%	2
France	77.0	79.7	4
Italy	77.4	78.4	5
Germany	76.7	75.0	7
Japan	68.7	67.8	6
U.S.	80.6	85.1	1
U.K.	80.9	83.8	3
SPEARMAN COEFFICIENT			+0.07
*Both government and private consumption			

The table also suggests that high-consumption ratios are positively related to low export or high import surpluses. This stands to reason. Nevertheless, the correlation between consumption and government deficits and between the trade balance and government deficits is essentially nil, which means that we cannot pin this result on fiscal policy.

A Weak Foundation

No, despite the stubborn insistence that cutting the deficit is the best way to raise the saving rate, its empirical foundation is weak. And its theoretical foundation is also open to argument. . . .

This debunking of the popular notions about budget deficits doesn't necessarily mean they are a good thing or even neutral to the economy. As a proxy for wasteful or unproductive government spending, they may ring the proper alarms. But that cannot be known absent other data, and measures to narrow deficits cannot be assumed to do more good than harm.

What this comparison does tell us is that placing the blame for the serious and stubborn problems facing the U.S. economy—high real interest rates, trade imbalances, low savings—on budget deficits doesn't hold up over an international sample. Is there some reason to think the U.S. case unique?

Peter L. Bernstein is a New York economic consultant and contributor to The Wall Street Journal.

Theodore Lownik Library
Illinois Benedictine College
Lisle, Illinois 60532

"Large changes in AFDC [Aid to Families with Dependent Children] may be closer than most people realize."

The Welfare Reform Bill: An Overview

Andrew Hacker

Both political parties and most legislators now agree that Aid to Families with Dependent Children, the program commonly called "welfare," needs radical reform. The Democratic platform pledges to "help people move from welfare to work." The Republicans also say they will "reform welfare to encourage work as the ticket that guarantees full participation in American life." Indeed, the GOP [Grand Old Party] now accepts that if single mothers are to become self-supporting, they will need subsidized child care. . . .

Large changes in AFDC may be closer than most people realize. Both chambers of Congress have passed a stringent "workfare" bill. . . . The belief behind the Family Security Act of 1988, which was largely drafted by Senator Daniel Patrick Moynihan, is that welfare creates a dependent underclass. Hence the view underlying the act that the time for solicitude has passed; discipline must be imposed. In particular, the statute's sponsors seek to change the outlook and behavior of the 3.3 million women now on the assistance rolls. Under its provisions, even mothers with preschool children will be forced to find jobs and support themselves. Given the emphasis on compulsion, it is appropriate to ask how justified this policy is, and what are the changes it may bring about.

Different Standards

Today most Americans feel that mothers of young children should not be deterred from working if that is what they want to do. Many wives choose not to work, and that too is viewed as a legitimate option. However, women who receive welfare tend to be judged by rather different standards. Under current AFDC rules, any single mother is allowed to apply for a stipend that will enable her to stay at home

with her children. Even so, states vary in their readiness to make these grants and in the amounts they offer. But it hardly needs remarking that the program is barely tolerated. In opinion polls most Americans rate it a failure, if not a scandal and a shame. Its initial purpose was to give needy citizens a respite, while they got back on their feet. However, the public is persuaded that too many recipients have made dependency a career: among all US families with children still at home, almost one in eight is now on the welfare rolls, while as recently as 1960 only one household in thirty-three was receiving AFDC.

The aim of the new Family Security Act, according to one of its sponsors, is "to get these people off the welfare rolls and onto the payrolls." Most of "these people" are women, since it is mothers or in some cases grandmothers who head 90 percent of all AFDC households. (In the others, a disabled or unemployed father may be present.) Since at least 1965, when he wrote *The Negro Family*, Daniel Patrick Moynihan has been proposing policies designed to end the poverty and pathologies associated with life on welfare. Moynihan ensured that the committee report would carry a detailed discussion of the act's major tenets. The report contains much useful information, as do the recent studies by David Ellwood of Harvard's Kennedy School and Isabel Sawhill at the Urban Institute in Washington. While they share most of Moynihan's concerns, they are less sanguine about some of his solutions.

A typical welfare family tends to be imagined as having half a dozen children, with the mother on the rolls for at least a dozen years. But as Table A shows this is one of several widely believed myths. In fact, three quarters of the AFDC households have one or two children, while fewer than 10 percent have as many as four. Only about a fourth of the parents have been receiving assistance for five or more

Andrew Hacker, "Getting Rough on the Poor," *The New York Review of Books*, October 13, 1988. Reprinted with permission from *The New York Review of Books.* Copyright © 1988 Nyrev, Inc.

years; and fewer than 10 percent have been on AFDC for over a decade.

At the same time, the figures support the general view that most recipients are black or Hispanic, out of proportion to their share of the population. This is to be expected, since within those minorities more households are headed by women. While black and Hispanic women comprise 21 percent of all women aged fifteen to forty-four, they account for 45 percent of all women who head households, and 55 percent of those receiving AFDC. To look at the figures another way, altogether 57 percent of Hispanic single mothers are on welfare, as are 55 percent of the comparable black group, while among single white women with children the proportion is 34 percent.

Unmarried Mothers

The figures also confirm popular concern that most of the mothers on AFDC have had their children out of wedlock. This itself is a significant shift from earlier years. Since 1973, the proportion of women receiving benefits because their husbands are unemployed, disabled, or deceased—generally seen as "legitimate" reasons—has declined by almost one half. And whereas the largest single category (46 percent) used to be women who were separated or divorced, it now consists of mothers who have never been married (52 percent; see Table A).

It is important to stress that most single mothers are not on welfare and in fact hold full-time jobs. Between 55 and 60 percent combine parenthood and employment, even when they have to settle for wages that barely support a household. Table B shows the incomes of the 6.3 million women who are single parents. That almost a quarter make more than $20,000 suggests how well they are coping, not only despite wage discrimination, but while caring for one or more youngsters, a burden borne by few fathers. That a further 27 percent earn between $10,000 and $20,000 tells us that they are not on welfare, since they have found they can make more on the job market. That so many single mothers have become self-supporting has bolstered the view that the rest should.

A further consequence of "men's liberation" is that fathers feel little obligation to support the children they have sired. Currently, 63 percent of single mothers receive no payments at all. And while 37 percent do, by no means all receive the agreed-upon sums. For those who do get checks, the yearly total averages $2,215, which must often be spread among several children. A California study found that men earning $45,000 were as likely to ignore court orders as those making $15,000. For these reasons, the Family Security Act intends to make delinquent fathers pick up a greater share of costs now covered by AFDC. If they do, the reasoning runs, the role of government will diminish, since it will only have to provide supplemental funds when parental support is inadequate.

As matters now stand, when child support is computed, the needs of the mother and the youngsters seem of secondary concern. The first factor is how much the father is judged "able" to pay. Judges, lawyers, and lawmakers generally presume that a man will need to keep 80 percent of his earnings for himself once he is on his own. This is not surprising since most of those involved in these decisions are men. Almost all divorced men remarry, moreover, and many start another round of children. So securing support for their first set can be uphill work. This may be why Isabel Sawhill sounds grateful for a recent Wisconsin law mandating minimum payments of 17 percent of the father's earnings. However, the law also sets a ceiling of 34 percent, no matter how many children the man has produced.

Some strains might be eased if more single mothers married or remarried. In most cases, adding a man's income to her own would double the family budget. However, such statistics as we have show that after the age of thirty, women face dismaying odds in the remarriage market. In the thirty-five-to-thirty-nine age group, only four in ten divorced women can expect to remarry. Former husbands face no similar hurdles, and usually choose younger women as their second mates.

"If government gets tougher about making fathers pay, then many men may try to deny paternity."

However, the fastest growing group of AFDC families consists of women who were not married when their babies were born and have not married anyone since. As Table A noted, in recent years these mothers and their children have risen from under a third of the welfare rolls to more than half. In most of these cases, the mothers conceived children with no expectation that a male parent would be taking up residence. In most such cases, moreover, those participating in making the baby tend to be young and poor. So far as the young men are concerned, David Ellwood writes in *Poor Support*, "fathering a child out of marriage is often seen as a badge of manhood, rather than a troubling set of new responsibilities." Thus fewer than 12 percent of out-of-wedlock fathers provide even token support payments. At the same time, girls choose to have and keep their babies; in their case, becoming a mother is often a badge of womanhood.

There is no way to live well on welfare. Even in the most generous states, stipends fall well below what the government defines as the poverty level. In

1986, annual cash allowances for a family with two children ranged from $1,380 in Alabama to $5,970 in Wisconsin, with the national average at $4,320. In 1986, it took an income of $8,740 for a family of three to escape the poverty category. Thus, as Table C shows, the typical AFDC stipend amounts to one seventh of the average American family income. Here, too, the states vary greatly, with the ratio of welfare to average US income ranging from 6 percent in Mississippi to 19 percent in Vermont. Even adding the value of food stamps, housing subsidies, and free routine medical treatment seldom raises a welfare family above the poverty line. Recent years have seen cutbacks in federal contributions, while states permit allowances to lag behind inflation. Whenever the government supports people on welfare, its manner of doing so ensures that they will be poor.

In fact, there are millions of women who were once on the welfare rolls and who are now self-supporting. Among them are wives who were not employed when their marriages broke up, and needed time to find a decent job. (Mothers can receive AFDC assistance while going to college.) Follow-up studies of the welfare rolls have shown that more than half of all recipients leave voluntarily before their third year.

Defaulting Fathers

The first part of Senator Moynihan's Family Security Act deals with defaulting fathers. Moynihan likes to cite a remark by the economist Stanley Lebergott: "Our national code of accepted behavior includes the right of men to propagate children, and then desert them." Lebergott calls this "men's liberation," which he finds more pronounced than its women's counterpart. In 1950 only 6 percent of all households lacked a resident male parent. Now the proportion is approaching 25 percent. When marriages break up, the children almost always end up living with the mother. We seldom give this much thought, since people tend to assume that a woman will be a more natural parent. Few fathers ask for even partial custody, since they take it as given that they cannot handle the job, a sentiment their wives usually share. (In the rare cases where a mother asks the father to take the children, she is seen as "walking out on the kids," an epithet we rarely hear nowadays when a father packs his bags.) Except in the relatively few cases of well-to-do fathers who pay adequate child support, having the children remain with the mother means that either she or the taxpayers end up paying most of the bills. And from what we hear, the taxpaying public is not very happy about footing these costs.

The legislators who drafted the Family Security bill apparently feel that if government gets tougher about making fathers pay, then many men may try to deny paternity. So the law will allow states to require "blood tests and genetic typing" for suspected fathers. That done, a federal bureau will then grade each state on its "paternity establishment

TABLE A

HOUSEHOLDS RECEIVING AID FOR DEPENDENT CHILDREN (AFDC)—1986

Number of Children		Age of Youngest Child	
One	43.4%	Under 3	38.4%
Two	30.8%	3 to 5	22.7%
Three	16.0%	6 to 11	24.3%
Four or More	9.8%	Over 11	14.5%

Time on AFDC		Race	
Under 7 Months	17.2%	White	39.7%
7 to 12 Months	12.7%	Black	40.7%
One to Two Years	17.3%	Hispanic	14.5%
Two to Five Years	26.8%	Asian	2.3%
Over Five Years	25.9%	Other or Unknown	2.7%

Mother's Age		Mother's Education	
21 or Younger	15.8%	Under Grade 12	47.4%
22 to 29	41.3%	High School Grad.	42.9%
30 to 39	30.3%	Some College	8.5%
40 or Older	12.7%	College Graduate	1.2%

Fathers of the Children

	1986	1973
Not Married to Mother	52.6%	31.5%
Divorced or Separated	31.7%	46.5%
Unemployed or Disabled	9.0%	14.3%
Deceased	1.7%	5.0%
Other or Unknown	5.1%	2.7%

Source: Department of Health and Human Services

TABLE B

INCOMES OF WOMEN WHO HEAD HOUSEHOLDS (1986)

$50,000 and Over	104,000	1.6%
$35,000 to $50,000	283,000	4.5%
$20,000 to $35,000	1,081,000	17.2%
$10,000 to $20,000	1,717,000	27.3%
Under $10,000	3,112,000	49.4%
	6,297,000	100.0%

Source: Bureau of the Census. Figures include women who are not currently married and have one or more children under the age of 18.

TABLE C

RATIO OF AVERAGE AFDC STIPEND TO MEDIAN FAMILY INCOME

Vermont	19.3%
Minnesota	19.0%
New York	18.3%
UNITED STATES	14.0%
Nevada	8.3%
Louisiana	7.6%
Mississippi	5.8%

percentage," listing how many fathers have been found for out-of-wedlock children. The states will also make fathers supply their Social Security numbers when a baby is born, to be used by agencies charged with finding delinquent dads. If some fathers protest that they are unable to help, since they are unemployed or poorly paid, states may order them to take part in training programs, so they may augment their earning power.

"Welfare reform needs strong political support."

This is an ambitious, if not intrusive, program, based on the premise that creating a human life carries long-term obligations. Unfortunately, many non-paying fathers simply lack the cash. A considerable number are among the 850,000 men now in our state and federal prisons or local jails. Others are drug addicts or homeless, or are youths who have yet to hold a steady job. While every dollar they pay will help, their prospects as providers are not very promising.

For this reason most of the provisions of the Family Security Act concern women. As has been noted, the aim is to get them off welfare and onto payrolls. First, mothers under twenty-two who have not graduated from high school will be obliged to complete a high school education. (They may do so, in some states, through special courses leading to a high school "equivalency" diploma.)

After that the act provides for "mandatory participation" in job-training programs for all women with children over the age of three. The 40 percent of current AFDC mothers with children under three would not have to take part, although many of them would still be required to leave the house and return to school. However, the bill also allows a state to limit its exemptions to women with children under the age of one; in that case, almost 90 percent of the women would have to attend school or training sessions. During this period, the bill says, AFDC allowances and medical benefits would continue, and some form—just what is not clear—of child care must be made available.

Presumptions of the Program

Upon completing a training program, a mother is presumed ready to go to work, and would be required to accept any "bona fide" offer of employment. The presumption is that such a job will pay wages that equal or exceed her welfare stipend, plus the value of food stamps and other services. The legislation also assumes that she will be able to make suitable arrangements for the care of her children. If a mother refuses to enter a training program or accept a "bona fide" job, she will be

removed from the AFDC rolls. To ensure that her children will not suffer, "protective payments" for them may be made to a "third party," bypassing the mother. Just who is meant by a "third party" and just how it will use the payments to care for a child, the act does not specify.

If all AFDC mothers with children over three will have to attend school or job-training sessions, and will have to take full-time jobs sooner or later, then 1.5 million new places for child care will have to be added to those now being used by working mothers. As it happens, the funding portion of the bill does not provide for new child-care services. Indeed it assumes that states will allow women on welfare to make much the same arrangements as currently employed mothers. The most recent census survey found that 31 percent of women who are now working leave their children at home, and 37 percent drop them off at someone else's house. Thus only 24 percent have them in child-care centers, nursery school, or kindergarten, and 8 percent take them along to work. (Nor do these figures include after-school arrangements for children in the elementary grades.)

But mothers on AFDC may be more likely to need organized child care. This raises questions of quantity, quality, and cost. For one thing, we hear that children from lower-income families need special attention to compensate for the limitations at home, and experts insist that child-care centers should have professional staffs, with one college-trained adult for every three or four children. Yet, curiously, the report on the bill assumes that $120 a month—$6 a working day—will provide suitable care for youngsters of preschool age. The centers that Harvard University runs for its clerical employees charge upward of $825 a month and the much-cited Swedish system has similar costs. What kind of child care will the Family Security Act be able to provide with only a small fraction of those budgets? And what kind of job training will the women get?

Little Confidence in the Program

Neither David Ellwood nor Isabel Sawhill expresses much confidence in the job-training programs currently available. Ellwood entitles his discussion "Big Promises, Modest Payoffs." As he sees it, "No carefully evaluated work-welfare programs have done more than put a tiny dent in the welfare caseloads." One project he cites spent close to $10,000 per participant; yet a follow-up study found that its graduates were averaging only $10 a week in wages more than a group that had not had any training. Sawhill reaches a similar conclusion about a five-state project. There, "employment rates for participants in the job-training programs were three to six percentage points higher than for other welfare recipients." Applying those figures to the whole AFDC population, she estimates that the proportion of households receiving assistance would drop by only five percentage points. As it turns out, much of the training has less to do with specific jobs than with basic literacy, and with such matters as dress and deportment, with knowing how to fill out forms or use an alarm clock. Those who are placed in jobs usually start out doing unskilled work. Nor is this surprising. According to Senator Moynihan, half of New York City's welfare mothers have never held any kind of job.

At the same time, there have been success stories. The most notable has been Massachusetts' education and training program ("ET"), which has had the strong support and attention of Governor Michael Dukakis. . . .

The Dukakis approach has tended to bypass the deeper problems of many welfare recipients. By choosing to concentrate on those most likely to turn in good performances, the program has built a record of success which can be displayed to the public. Still, you have to start somewhere. An experiment that begins with selective candidates usually comes up with tips and techniques that can be extended to people in more difficult situations. Certainly, a central lesson from Massachusetts is that welfare reform needs strong political support, something other pilot programs have lacked.

The Central Issue

The central issue posed in the controversy surrounding AFDC and the Moynihan bill is whether welfare should cease being an option for most single mothers. Under the Family Security bill, after a series of training sessions, women now on AFDC will be expected to become self-supporting, when presented with "bona fide" offers, however much they may object to those jobs. David Ellwood calls this "imposed work," and he condemns it on moral and practical grounds. He makes the point that only 27 percent of married mothers work throughout the year at full-time jobs. Moreover, he notes that as many as one in seven women on welfare have physical or mental disabilities that are not dissimilar to those afflicting men in similar surroundings.

"The ideological convictions many people have about the family and welfare are both intense and often contradictory."

So at this point several questions need sorting out. For most of us, work is not a matter of choice, since we must take some kind of job if we don't want to live in poverty. Nor do we always end up in positions we would have preferred or chosen. Even so, we do not call our employment involuntary or imposed. Why, then, should the withdrawal of AFDC benefits be seen as forcing people to work? After all, welfare allowances are unlike unemployment benefits and Social Security pensions in that they have never been viewed as entitlements. Welfare dependency is not a right but a dispensation bounded by rules. In response, Ellwood asks why we worry so much about the presumed indolence of unmarried mothers. He presents a different view:

> Single mothers ought to have the flexibility of wives. Some wives choose full-time work, some choose part-time work, and some do no market work at all. Many argue that single mothers should be able to make the same decisions.
> If we provide sufficient welfare support to give single mothers a full choice, we have to recognize that some single mothers will choose not to work at all, just as many wives do.

Ellwood proposes raising AFDC payments above the poverty line, so that single mothers who choose to stay at home will have a measure of comfort and self-respect. But might not this attract even more young unmarried women to the welfare rolls? It is not that teen-agers have babies in order to receive welfare funds. In fact, many actually want to become mothers, and the availability of AFDC allows them to act out that desire. Others are deterred because they know that welfare will keep them in poverty. Ellwood wishes to raise the stipends, for obvious humane reasons. A concern he does not address is that more generous allowances might encourage an even greater number of fifteen-year-olds to embark on motherhood.

The ideological convictions many people have about the family and welfare are both intense and often contradictory. There is, for example, the conservative position that a good mother will want to stay at home with her children. And as they grow older, she will be there when they return from school. Once the children are on their own, making a home for her husband is an honorable occupation. Nor are these wives and mothers considered "dependent" in any invidious sense: what they do is deemed to be full-time, productive work. Many husbands are willing, even eager, to support this arrangement.

Why, then, are conservatives so adamant about wanting to get single mothers out of their homes and onto full-time payrolls? The reasons become evident in *The New Consensus on Family and Welfare*, a report by the conservative think tank American Enterprise Institute in Washington. It opens with the axiom that "no able adult should be allowed voluntarily to take from the common good without also contributing to it." Married women who stay at home are not seen as a social cost, since they are supported by their husbands' earnings. But it is only if she has such support that a woman can be said to contribute to "the common good" by attending to her children.

So the American Enterprise Institute's position is that women who do not happen to have resident husbands should not ask to be subsidized by society. This stricture is most plainly applied to those who have children out of wedlock; women who engage in irresponsible reproduction should not ask for a free ride. Giving them money will only increase the tendency to reproduce. . . .

"The original aims of Aid to Families with Dependent Children were enlightened and humane."

At this point it is unrealistic to try to estimate the costs and gains of universal enforced work. Regarding Dukakis's ET program, the Massachusetts Taxpayers Foundation, a business research group, concluded that "the savings to the state far outrun the cost of the program." People who were once burdens under AFDC are now taxpaying workers. However, the report also notes that ET's outlays will rise if it moves beyond volunteers to less promising candidates. But here successes will bring offsetting savings, since long-term welfare recipients tend to incur more expenses. The Family Security Act asks for an annual appropriation of about $2.8 billion, to assist states in providing child care and other services. According to its sponsors, the bill will be "budget neutral," which means it will pay for itself and "not worsen the budget deficit." In addition to trimming the welfare rolls and creating more taxpayers, it predicts new revenues by securing greater payments from fathers. And it can be argued that as more families become self-supporting, the tenor of society will improve, so we will not have to pay so much for things like remedial education and prison cells.

Still, Ellwood's phrase "imposed work" lingers. The original aims of Aid to Families with Dependent Children were enlightened and humane. Women who found themselves on their own—most of them widowed or divorced—would be supported for a time while they created new lives. In addition, social workers would aid in this transition by advising on budget planning and other preparations. In fact, millions of single mothers still use welfare in this way, and they are not considered a problem. The difficulty is that too many others linger on the rolls for prolonged periods. Also, social work professionals have generally given up on this group. Hence the impulse to call AFDC a failure, and to remove it from the statute books.

Andrew Hacker teaches political science at Queens College in New York.

*"The Family Security Act is valuable as
a statement of principle. . . . The bill lays
the foundation for future legislation."*

viewpoint 5

The Welfare Reform Bill Will Be Beneficial

The New Republic

The *Washington Post* called it "a sweeping overhaul . . . a dramatic restructuring." The *New York Times* described it as "a break with the past" that could "stand the American welfare system on its head." It's hard to live up to that kind of billing, and the Family Security Act, passed overwhelmingly by the Senate, doesn't. Though supporters claim it will "break the cycle of dependency," the bill wouldn't substantially alter the mixture of obstacles and perverse incentives that has helped to get the underclass where it is today. This breathlessly awaited revision of the welfare system won't make much more than a dent in the culture of poverty.

Then again, a dent's better than nothing. . . . The Family Security Act is valuable as a statement of principle—not for what it does but for how it tries to do it. By endorsing the idea (in the abstract, anyway) that able-bodied adults should work for their welfare checks, the bill lays the foundation for future legislation of like philosophy and greater substance. Maybe five or ten years from now, this bill's sponsor, Senator Daniel Moynihan, will be able to say what he says about the current bill without having to cross his fingers: "We're going to take a payments program with a minor emphasis on jobs, and create a jobs program in which the income supplement is assumed to be temporary."

It's just as well, in a way, that effective welfare legislation is still years away. Any truly successful program will be much more expensive than conservatives would like and yet much harsher in its treatment of the poor than most liberals can now stomach. Washington will need a few years to warm up to the idea.

Opinion on welfare is delimited by two polar positions. First, there's the view that the only thing poor people need is access to the tools for success—basic education, job training, vocational counseling, and the like; given these bare necessities, they'll pull themselves up by the bootstraps. Then there's the view that what poor people need is to have a fire lit under them; if we can just cut away the safety net, and given them a stark choice between starvation and work, they'll find work. In the middle of these two views is workfare, which provides both carrot and stick. The government helps welfare recipients find a job, or actually offers them one, and then tells them the party's over; from now on, they'll have to work for their money, whether it comes from the government or a private employer.

No Dramatic Shift

At least that's what workfare means in theory. Most of the programs that now carry the label—the experimental programs that several states have created with the help of federal funds—are much less harsh. Nobody shows welfare recipients jobs and then tells them to work or die. They're usually just asked (literally, in some cases) to train for a job, look for a job, or, maybe, listen to tips on how to look for a job.

The Moynihan bill wouldn't shift this emphasis dramatically, in spite of the headlines about how it would "mandate work." True, it would make states compel welfare recipients to enter a program called JOBS [Job Opportunities and Basic Skills Training Program]. But states pleading lack of funds (as most could) wouldn't have to move more than a fifth of their welfare cases into the program. Besides, JOBS doesn't necessarily mean jobs. It consists mainly of remedial education, job training, counseling, and the like. Doubtless this will lead some people to work. But for others it will turn into an endless bureaucratic labyrinth, a game unto itself. No one expects the program to find jobs for more than one in 50 welfare cases annually.

The New Republic, "Gaining Ground," July 11, 1988. Reprinted by permission of THE NEW REPUBLIC, © 1988, The New Republic, Inc.

One reason Moynihan shied away from real workfare is that it costs real money. If you're going to insist that welfare recipients either take a job or lose their government check, you have to do two things. First, you must have a job to offer them. Since most of the 3.7 million adults on Aid to Families with Dependent Children (the main welfare program) aren't besieged by corporate headhunters, this means the government ultimately will either have to subsidize private sector jobs or serve as employer of last resort. Second, you must take care of preschool children while their parents are at work. And here we come to the crux of the workfare problem—the trickiest issue to handle morally and financially, and yet an issue that has to be handled if workfare is ever going to become a reality.

Conservatives who advocate a tough, all-stick, no-carrot workfare program like to talk as if the average federal welfare recipient were a 20-year-old man who spends his afternoons sitting on a park bench drinking Thunderbird when he could just as easily be pumping gas. In truth, the welfare rolls are populated mainly by husbandless mothers with young children. More than 80 percent of adults getting AFDC are women with no man around the house, and a large majority of these women have children under age six. So the only humane way to get welfare recipients into the workplace is to spend a bundle on day care.

A Laudable Attempt

This prospect thrills no one. Conservatives get edgy about the financial commitment, and liberals get squeamish about the moral question: Can a compassionate society force a 20-year-old high-school dropout with three kids to make her already bleak life even less bearable by adding 40 hours a week on an assembly line? The answer is, yes. And the reason isn't just that any workfare program of truly broad sweep must by definition reach single mothers of young children. The reason is that workfare is ideally suited to deliver an urgent message: don't have children unless you can support them. Forcing women to juggle motherhood with a job isn't the nicest way to drive this point home, but if the squalor of poverty hasn't done the trick, then nothing less will.

This is the point that virtually no politician wants to make audibly. Yes, workfare is supposed to help its clients in the long run, by getting them out of the poverty culture and into the job culture. But workfare is also a way to reduce the number of children born into the culture of poverty—which means that its purpose is partly to make having a baby on welfare an even more unpleasant experience than it is now. (The Moynihan bill also tries, laudably but to questionable effect, to perform the trickier task of discouraging *fathers* from creating

kids they can't or won't support. It provides for locating delinquent fathers and withholding child support from their paychecks.)

However they shy away from this stark formulation of the problem, politicians can't help but accept it once it's turned inside out: if mothers of young children are exempted from work requirements, then they're encouraged to have more children in order to stay exempted. Getting more babies born fatherless into the underclass isn't high on anyone's policy agenda. In other words, real workfare *can't help* but alter the incentives governing how many children are born into poverty—would you rather have more or fewer?

This logic leads quickly to the conclusion that even mothers of the *very* young shouldn't be exempt from work requirements. Consider the Moynihan bill. On the surface, its eligibility rules seem quite harsh. Whereas most states with "workfare" programs have exempted mothers with children under six, Moynihan exempts from the JOBS program only those with children under three (a threshold that leaves about half of welfare mothers exempt). This sounds like progress, but it may be a step backward. Previously you needed a baby every six years to keep your benefits without signing up for workfare. Now you need a baby every three years. To be sure, countervailing considerations exist, and all told a three-year-old threshold is almost certainly more effective than a six-year-old threshold. Still, the only way to make reasonably sure that a workfare system doesn't expand the welfare population is to exempt only mothers with children, say, six months old or younger.

> *"One of the least heralded aspects of the Family Security Act is among the most significant."*

For that reason, one of the least heralded aspects of the Family Security Act is among the most significant. The bill permits states to make the eligibility threshold quite low, so that only a child less than a year old will excuse a mother from the JOBS program. If a few states try this, and make an effort to skew the JOBS program away from training and toward real work, the result will be some genuine experiments in workfare.

It's natural to worry about the wisdom of taking children only a year old out of their homes. But in many of these cases, preschool children would be better off—nutritionally and educationally, at least—in well-run day-care centers than they are at home. Indeed, if the culture of poverty is what we believe it is—a realm in which despair and neglect often begin to take their toll in infancy—then the compassionate, liberal and conservative alike, should welcome this opportunity for early intervention. For conservatives, that will mean overcoming their general abhorrence of day care.

Solutions Cost Money

Exploiting the opportunity calls for day-care accommodations a cut above Acme child-care center—yet another reminder that a real solution to the welfare problem is going to cost money. How much? There's no telling, but it's safe to say that the sum will dwarf the $2.8 billion the Moynihan bill would spend over five years.

It's possible that the Family Security Act will improve conditions for the poor only enough to forestall further reform. As the baby boom generation heads toward middle age, and leaves a vacuum in its wake, the labor market will no doubt snap up some JOBS program graduates. That, in fact, is what Moynihan is explicitly counting on. But if in five years the underclass remains—even with that demographic boost—a large population, still isolated from the American economy, it will be time to come up with a welfare bill that deserves the headlines this one got.

The New Republic *is a weekly journal of opinion.*

"It is much easier to get into the welfare system than to get out of it."

The Welfare Reform Bill Will Be Harmful

Charles Murray

The last weekend before the welfare reform bill passed at the end of September 1988, the conference committee was still wrangling about that old bugaboo, the Welfare Cheat. Under the new legislation, welfare recipients who go to work will get a year of continued Medicaid and day-care benefits. What is to prevent a woman who has worked for a year from going back into the welfare system and reestablishing her eligibility? The conference committee solemnly devised a system whereby the secretary for health and human services must keep an eye on whether this is happening, so he can tell the Congress about it if it does, and then Congress can fix things.

What was ignored then, ignored during the earlier congressional debate, and continues to be ignored now except by a few die-hard right-wing pessimists, is that recycling into the system is not the biggest problem; the first cycle is. The problem lies not in the openings it will give to welfare cheats, but the trap it sets for the very opposite kind of person: the single mother who is working, supporting her family, and has managed to stay off the welfare rolls.

The intention of the provision of Medicaid and day-care benefits is to remove the disincentives for women who are already on welfare to get jobs. The provision uses exactly the same logic as the "30 and a third rule" adopted in 1967 that permitted welfare mothers who got a job to keep some of their welfare benefits as they earned money from jobs. In both cases, it is assumed that the best way to get people off welfare is through a material incentive. Why should a welfare mother get a job if it means giving up income or benefits?

The reason why the "30 and a third rule" backfired, and so will the provision of Medicaid and day-care benefits, is that there is no way to make it easier to get off welfare without also making it more attractive to get on welfare in the first place. Once again, we have adopted a policy on the basis of the people who already exhibit the problem we want to solve, while being blind to the effects of the policy on people who do not yet exhibit the problem.

The Potential for Backfire

The welfare-reform bill makes it easier for a woman already on welfare to take a job; that much is undisputed. This will have a positive effect on the subpopulation of welfare mothers who actively want to work full-time (not just answer "I want to work" when asked by a television reporter or social worker) and are job-ready (have the work habits that will enable them to keep a job once they get one).

Unfortunately, this profile of a hard-working, responsible woman who knows her way around the workplace is not typical of the chronic welfare recipient, who is likely to be a very young woman who has never worked and never had a husband. The hard-working, responsible women who are single mothers tend right now to be much more concentrated among another group, those who are already working and not on welfare. And therein lies the potential for backfire.

Consider such a woman. She is working and making do, even though it is not easy for her. She is rightly proud of maintaining her independence and she teaches her children to be proud of it, too. Under the former welfare law, whenever she lost her job she went out and got a new one as soon as possible—motivated both by her pride and by the fact that she was better off that way.

What happens under the new law when she loses her job? She has a choice. Either she can rush out as before to search for a new job. Or, if only she will swallow her pride and spend just a few months on welfare, then get a job, she can get both day-care

Charles Murray, "New Welfare Bill, New Welfare Cheats," *The Wall Street Journal*, October 13, 1988. Reprinted with permission of The Wall Street Journal © 1989 Dow Jones & Company, Inc. All rights reserved.

and Medicaid benefits. It will take a very strongminded woman indeed to avoid this seductive reasoning: "I will still be just as before, working for my living. The only difference will be that I'll have gotten these extra benefits. Nothing else will have changed."

Easier To Quit Working

But it is much easier to get into the welfare system than to get out of it, and many women who expect to go back to work will find that, for one reason or another, they're going to put it off a little. When they do get jobs, they will find it easier to quit. When they work long enough to come to the end of their child-care and Medicaid, the arguments for conveniently losing their jobs at that point and beginning the cycle over again will be self-evident—and it will turn out they can do so, because neither the Congress nor the secretary of health and human services is going to cut off benefits to a woman with children under any circumstances. It has never happened, never will.

On a pragmatic level, the implication is that the number of AFDC [Aid to Families with Dependent Children] families, which has been moving within a narrow range of 3.6 million to 3.8 million during the 1980s, may be expected to rise. It will rise in part just because of the requirement in the welfare-reform bill that makes two-parent families eligible for AFDC payments in all 50 states, but I will venture the more specific prediction that the number of female-headed families receiving AFDC will increase as well, and increase out of proportion to the growth of the general population.

"The welfare system has been moving in the wrong direction since 1932."

In 1986, about 3.5 million single mothers were on the welfare rolls. Everything we know about the past results of training programs for chronic welfare recipients tells us that very few of them will be moved off the rolls by the new bill. In that same year of 1986, 2.6 million single mothers were not on the welfare rolls. All except the firmly middle class of those 2.6 million will become potential new recruits to welfare as a means of qualifying for a year of very valuable benefits.

Much more important than the numbers: The woman who thinks "nothing else will have changed" if she goes on welfare and then goes back to work will find she was wrong. She formerly was accomplishing something very important, for both herself and her children, the accomplishment of being a competent, independent adult. Now she will have become another game-player. The lesson she passes on to her children will no longer be, "Stand on your own two feet," but, "Beat the system."

The social-democratic solution is to get rid of such disincentives by making free day-care available to everyone, making free medical coverage available to everyone, and ultimately making the concept of a "competent, independent adult" as fuzzy as possible. In this regard, a second specific prediction is in order. Within a few years it will become politically intolerable that women lose these benefits just because they have been off welfare for more than a year, and both benefits will become entitlements for all women up to the borders of the middle class.

In the grand scheme of things, these predictions do not spell disaster. They will constitute changes in degree, not in kind. But for those of us who believe that the welfare system has been moving in the wrong direction since 1932, the prospect is nonetheless depressing. The reason why welfare is bad is not because it costs too much, not because it "undermines the work ethic," but because it is intrinsically at odds with the way human beings come to live satisfying lives. The welfare reformers wanted to validate this truth, but will succeed only in obscuring it.

Charles Murray is a Bradley Fellow at the Manhattan Institute for Policy Research.

Requiring Welfare Recipients To Work: An Overview

Michael Wiseman

Work has been a prominent issue in the national debate over welfare policy for more than twenty years. Most Americans seem to agree that adults who are capable of working should, if possible, contribute to the support of themselves and their dependents. But substantial disagreement arises over the way, if any, this obligation should be imposed by society, the extent to which those who are not self-supporting are capable of becoming so, and the ability of government to help in attaining this end. All of these questions have resurfaced in connection with discussions of "workfare," that is, welfare reforms that link income maintenance to employment programs.

Many of the issues in the workfare debate involve social values and not empirical problems. But workfare proposals also raise practical issues of policy, and here the outcomes of actual workfare programs and efforts at training poor people for jobs provide important lessons. . . . Welfare work programs offer a useful opportunity for incremental welfare reform, but unanswered questions about the organization and consequences of such programs necessitate a cautious approach to program development and merchandising.

The Work Requirement Debate

Current workfare programs all involve something more than a work requirement. Virtually all create a new sense of obligation to undertake some activity in exchange for benefits. Requiring work is the traditional way of doing this. In its simplest form, the work requirement is a standard of eligibility for assistance: unless the potential recipient is willing to work for some agency of the state, benefits are denied. Generally, the benefits involve more than

Michael Wiseman, "Workfare and Welfare Reform," in *Beyond Welfare*, Harrell R. Rodgers, ed. Armonk, NY: M.E. Sharpe, Inc., 1988. Reprinted by permission of M.E. Sharpe, Inc., Armonk, New York 10504.

wages, since most income maintenance schemes tailor payments to factors such as household size.

Making the poor work for relief has a long (and generally sordid) history going back to the English Henrician Poor Law of 1536 ("the Act for the Punishment of Sturdy Vagabonds and Beggars"). This history reinforces opposition to such policies.

The Case for Work Requirements

Five interrelated arguments might be cited as support for requiring that needy persons work for benefits.

(1) *A work requirement is an effective test of need.* Most eligibility tests for public assistance involve current income, assets, or both. But need, at least in the abstract, is a matter not of what income is, but of what it could be. The willingness of the poor to work for benefits seems, for most people, to be a convincing demonstration of the absence of alternatives. This "needs effect" is ongoing. A work requirement creates incentives for job finding, or location of other resources, if opportunities arise. As such, it substitutes for the financial incentives that have been incorporated in welfare programs to encourage work.

(2) *Work requirements reduce welfare costs.* Costs are reduced in two ways. Work programs offset payments costs by the value of the product of the work recipients do. Costs are also lowered by caseload reductions that result from the "needs effect" already cited.

(3) *Work programs can preserve or enhance skills and contribute to employability.* The longer people are out of the labor force, the greater the difficulty they are likely to experience in obtaining and holding a job. Work, even in special jobs, may forestall this effect; and for recipients with no work history, workfare provides job experience.

(4) *Work requirements make welfare more equitable.* It has been an abiding principle of welfare reform

efforts that persons who work should be better off financially than those who do not work. But well-being involves both money income and time. While households of the working poor not receiving assistance may have higher money incomes than comparable welfare-dependent families without earners, they may be worse off, both because they do not get the in-kind benefits available to welfare recipients (such as Medicaid) and because welfare recipients do not have to work outside the home. This differential may be particularly evident to single parents who struggle to find sufficient time for both work and childrearing.

(5) *Work requirements enhance political support for public assistance.* Survey data consistently indicate more generous public response to the needs of the working than the nonworking poor. Recent research suggests that this attitude carries over to differentiation on the basis of how resolutely the unemployed recipients are trying to find a job. Also, some studies indicate that the generosity of state welfare benefits is inversely related to expected total welfare costs. Work programs thus lay the political foundation for higher basic benefit levels by assuring work effort and by reducing the caseload that will result from any given benefit standard.

The Case Against Work Requirements

Work requirements for welfare recipients are anathema to many persons concerned about social-welfare policy. Such programs, it is asserted, stigmatize the poor. Required work is therefore counter to the traditional focus of reform efforts, which has been on the development of systems of universal income support, such as the negative income tax, that provide nonintrusive cash assistance based on money income alone.

Opponents also deny the validity of the arguments that constitute the case for mandatory work requirements. The needs test argument may be rejected, it is claimed, because in welfare programs such as Aid to Families with Dependent Children (AFDC), eligibility already requires low or nonexistent income, very few assets, and, for many recipients, mandatory work registration and job search. The gains from eliminating a few persons unwilling to work from welfare rolls would be offset by the additional burden placed upon the majority of the genuinely needy and, in addition, upon the dependents of those who, for whatever reason, would refuse to accept mandated jobs. As for the skills argument, unless the jobs provided are skill-intensive (and therefore costly to provide), it seems unlikely that labor alone will enhance a recipient's job readiness.

Opposition to the incentives and equity arguments for work requirements turns in part on perceptions of the circumstances of welfare recipients. If welfare cases stay open only for relatively short periods of

time and occur because of events beyond people's immediate control—loss of jobs, for example—then welfare serves an insurance function, and the problem of dependency has its origin in the supply of jobs, and not recipients' unwillingness to work. Under these circumstances a work program might even lengthen welfare spells by interfering with the search for new, unsubsidized employment. Political support is a matter of education; if people correctly understand the circumstances of the needy, support will be forthcoming.

"It is now possible to combine under the general workfare label any program in which income maintenance is explicitly linked to employment preparation."

Opponents of mandated employment programs also tend to emphasize the cost of work-program operation. An effective work mandate requires a job-of-last-resort for all who are eligible. To guarantee the virtues of the program, such jobs must produce useful output (to offset costs), enhance skills (to improve employability), and be organized in the expectation of rapid employee turnover. These requirements call for considerable capital and managerial commitment as well as innovation. Without novelty, it is likely that the jobs, especially the more valuable jobs, will replicate work done by regular employees of public or private organizations and therefore incur charges of displacement. Attempts at implementation of small-scale work requirements in the 1970s in California, Massachusetts, and Minnesota were plagued with administrative problems and failed to achieve employment targets. Given the institutional and social constraints under which welfare policy must operate, critics argue, such programs, even if desirable, are simply not administratively feasible.

Recent Developments

Despite reservations such as those outlined above, interest in workfare grows. This is a product of a more inclusive definition, opportunities created by legislation, and other developments.

One of the most significant aspects of the evolution of thinking about work-welfare programs is the changing definition of workfare. In 1972, when then-Governor Ronald Reagan introduced the original Community Work Experience Program in California, workfare meant working in return for welfare payments. Fifteen years later the workfare designation has become much more broadly applicable, encompassing an obligation for job search or training, and not just work in public parks. The reason for this is in part political: some consider making needy people look for work a more palatable alternative than making them cut weeds. But the change also reflects the idea that the essence of a work requirement is not what you do, but whether you are *obligated* to do it. Thus it is now possible to combine under the general workfare label any program in which income maintenance is explicitly linked to employment preparation. Today, workfare programs are not simply systems that mandate that recipients work in exchange for benefits. Rather, they tend to entail processes, steps certain welfare-receiving adults are expected to take in connection with benefit receipt.

Legislation

The catalyst for new attention to workfare was the Omnibus Budget Reconciliation Act of 1981 (OBRA). OBRA allowed states to establish mandatory Community Work Experience Programs (CWEP). Adults receiving AFDC could be required to participate in CWEP training and "work experience" activities "to assist them to move into regular employment."

In addition to CWEP, OBRA and subsequent legislation made other important additions to the toolkit for work-related welfare changes. Many of these opportunities are related to the Work Incentive Program (WIN).

WIN was established by Congress in 1967 to furnish training programs and other employment-related assistance to welfare recipients. As originally designed, the program featured a dual administrative structure at both federal and state levels. On the one hand, the U.S. Department of Labor and the various state employment services handled work registration and training activities. On the other, the welfare application, approval, and payments system is the province of the U.S. Department of Health and Human Services and state income-maintenance units. WIN mandated that certain adult recipients—mothers without preschool children in single-parent families, and the unemployed principal earner (usually the father) in two-parent families—register with the WIN program as a condition of receiving welfare. In practice the participation requirement has not been meaningful, for shortages of staff and funds and coordination problems created by WIN itself have meant that two-thirds or more of those who register for WIN received no services. In theory able-bodied adults without transportation problems or childcare problems who refused to accept job referrals generated through WIN or to participate in training could be "sanctioned" by reduction of welfare grants. In practice this has rarely occurred. Some critics of WIN point to this as evidence of lack of effort. It is claimed that if WIN requirements were enforced for a larger share of recipients, performance would be improved.

OBRA granted states the option of setting up WIN "demonstrations" in which the WIN program is administered solely by welfare agencies, which in turn contract with the state employment services for employment-related activities for clients. The option potentially allows states to avoid the administrative problems created by dual administration of the WIN program. Legislation passed in 1982 allows states to require AFDC applicants and recipients who meet WIN eligibility criteria to participate in a program of job search of up to eight weeks at the time of accession to AFDC, and up to eight weeks per year thereafter. States may target the requirement to subsets of the WIN registrant pool. The legislation includes federal support for transportation and other costs incurred. OBRA and the Deficit Reduction Act of 1984 authorized states to set up programs whereby AFDC funds could be used for limited periods to subsidize employment for welfare recipients placed in entry-level positions in nonprofit agencies and in private firms.

"The new workfare programs attempt to increase participation rates to the point where virtually all eligible adults meeting specified criteria participate."

While OBRA gave states the workfare toolkit, four other developments provided the "building permit." One is resumption of growth of the AFDC caseload after the reductions brought about by other OBRA provisions. Work programs, it is suggested, could reverse this trend. Burgeoning popular and scholarly concern over long-term welfare dependency and the associated development of a socially isolated underclass in the poorest areas of the nation's cities is a second influence. Some argue that work programs are important for reintegration of this group with the rest of society. The third is the growing attention given arguments that the AFDC system itself has contributed to poverty and welfare dependence by discouraging work. As already discussed, work incentives are a major part of the case for work requirements. Finally, and perhaps of greatest importance, work and welfare programs have proved to be good politics, both for Republican conservatives such as Governor George Deukmejian of California and for new liberal Democratic leaders such as Governor Michael Dukakis of Massachusetts.

The New Workfare

All of the new work-welfare schemes are amalgamations of AFDC and the old WIN with the tools presented by the new legislation. A representative program is set out in Figure 1, which charts steps that might be required of certain recipient-family adults in a new workfare program. These steps are as follows. First, on acceptance (sometimes on application) for welfare, the recipient registers for the workfare program and goes through a preliminary screening. Under arrangements fostered by the WIN demonstration office, this is done in immediate conjunction with welfare application. If a recipient is prevented from seeking employment for certain specified reasons, particularly because of lack of childcare, an attempt is made to provide the needed services in order to certify the recipient as employment-ready. Sometimes employment-readiness requires motivational counseling and training in interview techniques.

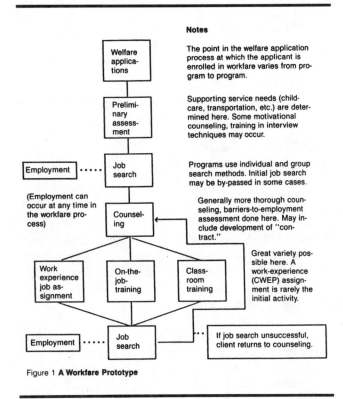

Notes

The point in the welfare application process at which the applicant is enrolled in workfare varies from program to program.

Supporting service needs (child-care, transportation, etc.) are determined here. Some motivational counseling, training in interview techniques may occur.

Programs use individual and group search methods. Initial job search may be by-passed in some cases.

Generally more thorough counseling, barriers-to-employment assessment done here. May include development of "contract."

Great variety possible here. A work-experience (CWEP) assignment is rarely the initial activity.

If job search unsuccessful, client returns to counseling.

Figure 1 **A Workfare Prototype**

When the recipient is judged employment-ready, step two is an organized job-search effort. Organization varies, but a common approach involves "job club" techniques in which the adult joins other recipients at a regular time to make phone calls and plot job-finding strategies under the tutelage of a professional placement counselor.

If the job-search effort fails, the participant goes on to more intensive counseling and more detailed investigation of possible alternatives for employability enhancement. At this point the recipient gains access to a set of classroom or on-the-job training programs, becomes eligible for a subsidized job placement, or in some cases, may be assigned to community work. A plan is developed for recipient participation in some program. In general recipients are not paid for any of these activities, or where pay is received it is in lieu of the

welfare payment. Funding for the services may come from a variety of sources; some of the training may be obtained from the local Private Industry Council using federal funds provided through the Jobs Training Partnership Act.

Skepticism

After program completion the recipient again participates in job search, followed by counseling, and so on.

Of course, actual workfare programs differ in detail from this model. Some states have been very slow in taking advantage of the new options. For example, in the spring of 1987 only 26 states were operating WIN demonstrations; 27 states were exercising the job-search option; 25 states had CWEP in at least one local area; and just 15 states were experimenting with grant diversion/work supplementation programs. Nonetheless, interest in such programs, and the scale of proposals, was growing rapidly, and most programs appear to be evolving toward something like the model presented in Figure 1.

Experience with the difficulty of reforming welfare leads to skepticism about any policy posed as a solution to problems as diverse as reducing the long-time welfare dependency of the poor and assuring the long-time incumbency of politicians. Also, as critics are quick to point out, Figure 1 is a long way from the old-fashioned notion that the best welfare program is a job of last resort. While the new programs often do incorporate work requirements, they also often commit substantial additional resources. Perhaps most importantly, they manifest a change in philosophy. Whereas employment-related activities have long been part of welfare, most programs have been small relative to the eligible population and, because of this, participation was largely optional for most recipients. The new workfare programs attempt to increase participation rates to the point where virtually all eligible adults meeting specified criteria participate. Workfare changes the nature of the welfare bargain. It does this not simply by conditioning welfare receipt on work, as in the simplest of work requirements, but by conditioning welfare receipt on an active program of preparation for self-support. Willingness to participate in such efforts in effect becomes a test of need for public assistance. The result is intended to make efforts at self-support an obligatory concomitant of receipt of public assistance, and delivery of employment-related services an obligatory concomitant of welfare system operation.

Michael Wiseman is an associate professor of economics at the University of California at Berkeley.

Welfare Recipients Should Be Required To Work

Lawrence M. Mead

Work for welfare recipients has suddenly become a hot topic in Washington. Politicians say they want to place more dependent adults in training or employment programs. Some even claim we can turn welfare into "workfare," as President Nixon promised when he proposed his own ill-fated welfare reform nearly 20 years ago. The idea is popular, as the public has long wanted recipients to do more to help themselves. . . .

Liberal reformers presume that welfare recipients fail to work because they face special "barriers," notably a lack of jobs, child-care, and training opportunities. If government provided more of these things, liberals assert, welfare work levels would rise. That is a misconception. Research has shown that the presumed impediments rarely keep people from working, at least in low-skilled, low-paid jobs. The main reason for nonwork, rather, is the reluctance of many recipients to take such jobs. The main task of welfare work policy is to overcome that reluctance. While this probably requires some new services, it above all requires more clear-cut *requirements* that recipients work in return for benefits. Those who favor increased benefits are seeking not so much to promote work as to advance the traditional liberal interest in social equality.

Reform, to be effective, must abandon the illusion that work is impossible for the poor. The major obstacles to welfare employment lie in the minds of the poor, and in the permissive attitudes of federal legislators. Welfare policymakers must believe what the facts show—work can be required of the majority of adult recipients.

The work issue has come to the fore for a good reason: Nonwork is the immediate cause of much poverty and dependency today. There is still a tendency to see the poor simply as victims entitled to government redress. That view is most plausible for the elderly and disabled poor, whom society does not expect to work. But, it is implausible for families headed by able-bodied people of working age, whom society does expect to work.

This article focuses primarily on working-age adults; I do not suggest that children, the elderly, or the disabled should work. I also recognize that much of poverty is transient, and that half of all welfare cases leave the rolls in under two years. I am speaking here mainly of the long-term cases, and especially about the welfare mothers and absent fathers whose reluctance to work helps create entrenched dependency. . . .

Changed Social Norms

Liberal reformers say that welfare mothers face special difficulties in working. After all, AFDC [Aid to Families with Dependent Children] was first instituted in 1935 on the supposition that mothers heading families were unemployable. They were supposed to stay home and raise their children. If we now demand that they work, government must first guarantee them child-care.

But the surge of women into jobs has changed social norms. Welfare mothers can no longer be seen as unemployable now that more than half of female family heads with children under 18 are working, nearly three-quarters of them full-time. For divorced and separated mothers like those on AFDC, the working proportion is nearly two-thirds. Welfare mothers are distinctly out of step. Only about 15 percent of them worked in the 13 years prior to the 1981 cuts in AFDC eligibility, which removed most working mothers from the rolls. This was so even though the mothers were often more employable during that period—younger, better-educated, and with fewer children (over 70 percent now have only one or two).

"Jobs for the Welfare Poor," by Lawrence M. Mead is reprinted from *Policy Review* Issue #43 (or Winter 1988). *Policy Review* is a publication of The Heritage Foundation, 214 Massachusetts Avenue NE, Washington, DC, 20002.

While children certainly make work difficult for mothers, they are not the hard-and-fast barrier that is often supposed. In fact, as high a proportion of single mothers work as do single women without children. Even young children are not prohibitive. Welfare mothers with pre-school children may be no less likely to work their way off the rolls than those with older children, and two-thirds of mothers who leave welfare this way still have children at home.

Government Child Care

Working mothers certainly need child-care, but they seldom rely on organized facilities such as government child-care centers. Only 9 percent of primary child-care arrangements by working parents involved day-care centers or nursery schools in 1984-85. Even for the most dependent group, single mothers with children under 5, it was only 27 percent. Overwhelmingly, the parents rely on less formal arrangements, chiefly care by friends or relatives, either in their own homes or that of the caretaker.

Apparently, they arrange care fairly easily, as fewer than 6 percent of working mothers in a given month lose time on the job because of problems with their child-care arrangements. In only 10 percent of cases is the availability of care critical to a mother seeking work; finding the right job is much more important.

Child-care advocates claim that the parents would use more center care if it were available. But most mothers prefer informal arrangements, probably because they have more control over them. When government has offered free care in centers as part of social experiments, it has sometimes gone untaken. Informal care is also much less costly than center care, which must satisfy elaborate government staffing and licensing rules.

There appears, in fact, to be little unmet need for child-care. That is why proposals for a national day-care program covering the general population have always failed. Of course, government must *pay* for care for welfare mothers if it wants them to work. It already does this, usually by adjusting the mother's grant, while they are on welfare. More funding for transitional care after they leave welfare may be needed. But government need not provide the care in its own facilities.

Finally, liberal reformers say that adult recipients can be expected to work only if they first receive training to raise their skills and earnings. Otherwise, they will fail to get jobs or, if they do get them, will not earn enough to get off welfare or out of poverty. That is the rationale behind the heavy emphasis on training in the Democratic reform plans.

The benefits of training have been deduced from evaluations of some of the post-1981 work programs by the Manpower Demonstration Research Corporation (MDRC). These suggest that well-run training and jobs programs for recipients have the potential to raise their income by as much as 25 percent, as well as reduce dependency.

But training is easily oversold. The earnings gains in even the best training programs are limited, seldom enough to get welfare families entirely out of poverty or off welfare. Furthermore, "training" can be a misnomer, as few programs raise the skills of adults on welfare, most of whom have shown little ability to learn in school. The main impact of training programs is not on job quality but on motivation—on causing the clients to work *more hours* in the rudimentary jobs they are already able to get.

The best training programs tend to be highly authoritative, aimed at impressing on clients a responsibility to work at whatever job they can get. Nondirective programs can actually *depress* work effort, as clients embark on unrealistic training programs for "better" jobs at the expense of immediate employment. Welfare employment programs have made that mistake in the past. They overinvested in training, only to see very few trainees go to work in available jobs. The current liberal reform proposals would repeat that error.

Nor is training usually necessary for work. In fact, welfare mothers average 2.6 years of work experience since they left school. Many work "off-the-books" while they are on welfare, a dodge that work requirements help to detect. Their problem is seldom that they are literally unemployable but rather that they do not work *consistently*.

"Work where government bears all the burdens without holding the employee accountable for performance is not really work. It is simply another form of welfare."

This is not to say that work is easy for welfare mothers, or for anyone. Serious effort is required to find a job and to arrange one's private life for work. But these burdens do not seem notably greater for the poor and dependent than they are for other low-skilled people. What liberal reformers call "barriers" are mostly the ordinary demands of employment—demands that most working Americans cope with every day. Welfare adults face serious difficulties landing well-paid jobs, but not low-paid ones. Moreover, if the benefits provided in liberal reform bills were really necessary to employment, how do so many other low-skilled workers do without them?

Government could perhaps overwhelm these so-called barriers with benefits, guaranteeing jobs, child-care, and training especially for the poor and dependent. But to do that would be unfair to the many other Americans who already work in menial jobs without special assistance. It would also be ineffective in integrating the poor, because they would not earn the respect of others. Work where government bears all the burdens without holding the employee accountable for performance is not really work. It is simply another form of welfare. . . .

Why Work Must Be Required

But work policies fail when discipline cannot be assumed. Employment programs aimed specifically at the poor and disadvantaged have shown little impact, mainly because they asked, and got, little commitment from their clients. The error of federal incentives, training, and jobs programs was that they offered only benefits in one form or another, without firm work requirements. All attempted, one way or another, to raise wages per working hours, as if low wages were the major cause of poverty. None directly confronted the greater problem—the low number of hours the poor work. All assumed that benefits of some sort could entice the jobless poor to work more. All assumed that opportunity was the main problem, instead of motivation.

Unfortunately, that assumption is invalid. The long-term poor seem to be a remarkably *un*responsive group. Their work levels have remained low for a generation, in good times and bad, in the face of a succession of programs meant to inspire or reward work. In fact, the opportunities and incentives the poor have to get ahead are already great, as shown by the recent success of Asian immigrants. No government benefit could add to that opportunity very much. There is now no reason to suppose that any reform that only changes incentives will get much response.

None of the work benefits directly mandated higher work levels. None set any standards for work effort. No training or jobs program required that clients be working, or have worked, in existing jobs in order to qualify for benefits. Accordingly, the programs operated more as substitutes for work than as preparations for it. By entering them, clients could avoid coming to terms with the low-skilled jobs that were all they could usually get, even after training. "Employment" programs thus undercut rather than affirmed the work norm.

Reluctantly, policymakers have begun to accept that work must be enforced as are other civilities such as obedience to the law or tax payment. Work serves important social values, particularly provision of higher income and social integration. So dependent adults should be required to work, even if—due to other income from families or programs—their immediate preferences are otherwise. Rather than be offered further opportunities and rewards for working, they should simply be *required* to work in return for the income they are already getting.

They should face the demands for performance, for reciprocity, that nondependent Americans face every day.

Requirements approach the work problem as one of enforcement rather than barriers. Whereas the barriers theory says the poor are blocked from work and need greater freedom, the enforcement theory says they are in some ways too free. The solution to the work problem lies in *obligation*, not in freedom.

Requirements suit the irresolute mentality of the poor. They *want* to work but feel they *cannot*. Enforcement operates to close the gap between the work norm and actual behavior, and changes work from an aspiration to an obligation. It places the employable poor in a structure, combining supports and requirements, where they find that they must do what they always wanted, which is to work. . . .

"Work must be enforced as are other civilities such as obedience to the law or tax payment."

The rationale for workfare is simply that it has drawn more response from the dependent than any other measure. It has raised actual work effort, where benefits expanded only opportunities. Poor adults seem to respond more strongly to public authority than they ever did to incentives. The effect is especially great while clients are actually in the program, but some of it persists afterwards, showing up as higher earnings months later. That achievement outweighs the economic gains of the programs, as it suggests how the welfare work problem might finally be solved.

An effective welfare reform should define welfare mothers as employable when their youngest children are three or older, rather than six as now mandated. But above all it should require that higher proportions of the employable recipients, however defined, be genuinely working, looking for work, or training as a condition of eligibility for welfare. For teen-aged mothers, the obligation would be to stay in school until graduation. I would set an initial participation target of 50 percent, phased in over several years, and then see if higher levels were feasible. Child-care would be financed, but mothers would be required to arrange their own unless they could show that this was impossible. Some training would be included, but it would be confined to clients who were working, at least part-time, or who had a recent work record. Workfare policy should rely on government employment only when job search efforts in the private sector proved fruitless. Any government workfare jobs should have clear-cut performance standards, for which the workfare employees are held accountable.

Why, then, do liberals resist mandating higher participation levels? In part, no doubt, because the idea of serious work requirements strikes many as coercive. It also cuts against the pork-barrel proclivities of federal politics. Federal politicians would much rather give deserving groups good things than tell them how to behave. Until recently, even conservative politicians shared that attitude. They simply wanted fewer benefits than liberals. They counted on the private sector to enforce social mores such as the desire to work. Only the sharpening of the social problem has forced both sides to confront the need for functioning standards within welfare.

Liberals, in addition, resist accepting that the poor should be held responsible in any sense for their behavior. For a generation, they have defined the poor as victims. They assigned the responsibility for change entirely to government. Workfare, however, would share that onus between the poor adult and government. The two would work together to overcome dependency, the one by working more, the other by providing necessary support services. There seems no other way to change the dysfunctional patterns that now create poverty. Yet for welfare advocates, whose identity is wrapped up in claim-making, even a division of responsibility is anathema. Pressures from these groups explain why the Democratic plans give only lip service to requirements.

Greater than these difficulties, however, is the fact that the jobs commonly available to the poor are usually not very nice. For most recipients, relatively "dirty work" is the only realistic alternative to welfare. They must work in unappealing jobs, or not at all. No government policy can improve that choice very much. If training or government jobs could somehow qualify the poor for "better" positions, a policy requiring work would be less contentious. But they can do this only for a few. Work policy cannot be based on that hope, or higher work levels will never be achieved.

Good Jobs

Most conservatives would accept those alternatives and enforce work. Most liberals reject them as a Hobson's choice. They want the poor to work—but only in "good" jobs. Their upset is that "dirty work" would not advance the goal of equality as they understand it—a more equal distribution of income and status in the United States. Low-paid jobs are enough to lift most families off welfare and out of poverty, if all adults work; but they would not assure middle-class incomes. Even if working, many of today's poor, like yesterday's, would have to wait for "success" in their children's lives rather than their own.

Concretely, the issue often comes down to whether the *first* job that recipients take must be a good one.

Conservatives tend to say not. They accept that entry-level jobs are usually low-paid. The unskilled should take such jobs to accumulate a work record, after which they can qualify for "better" positions. Meanwhile, they can count on supplementation from welfare or other family members. This is acceptable because most workers in entry-level jobs are young. But advocate groups demand that available jobs be good enough to take the family off welfare and out of poverty immediately. Mainstream income cannot require any apprenticeship. Better to be idle and dependent than working-poor. For them, the low-paying, first job is as much of a "barrier" to employment as if no jobs existed at all.

"We must require equal obligations of the poor as well as assure them equal rights."

The drive for equality shapes the positions liberals take even on issues of fact. Many, for instance, concede tacitly that jobs of a menial kind are usually accessible to the poor. They question, rather, whether "good," "decent," or "meaningful" jobs are available—a very different thing. By fudging whether they mean jobs or good jobs, they often avoid facing up to the evidence that work is already widely available. Bradley Schiller has written, for example, that to overcome poverty, government must assure "an abundance of jobs—jobs that provide decent wages and advancement opportunity," as if these were the same thing. Such comments suggest that the real dispute in work policy is about equality, not opportunity. . . .

The work problem *is* a problem of participation, not of equality. The great question is how to get more of the employable poor to participate in the economy, in any kind of job, not how to improve those jobs. . . .

To be equal in America means to possess the same essential rights *and* obligations as other people. . . .

We must require equal obligations of the poor as well as assure them equal rights if they are to be truly integrated. To do that should be the purpose of welfare reform.

Lawrence M. Mead is associate professor of politics at New York University. He is author of Beyond Entitlement: The Social Obligations of Citizenship.

"There is little evidence that any of the commonly used welfare-to-work strategies can lead to lasting independence for most AFDC parents."

viewpoint 9

Requiring Welfare Recipients To Work Is Ineffective

Joan Walsh

Denise Richards traded her welfare check for a paycheck almost a year ago and hasn't looked back. She hasn't had the time. Small luxuries like quiet thought, a social life, and spending time with her four kids have been sacrificed in her transformation from Welfare Mother to Single Supermom.

Richards, 28, works as an operating room technician at Boston's Brigham and Women's Hospital. Her $9-an-hour job brings home twice what her monthly welfare grant did, though the loss of food stamps and rent subsidies narrows the financial difference between welfare and work. Still, she is glad to be working. As a high school dropout who had her first child as a teen, Richards fits the profile of the long-term welfare recipient—single mothers with so many obstacles to employment that Aid to Families with Dependent Children (AFDC) seems their only means of survival.

Through Massachusetts's Employment and Training Choices (ET), Richards finished her high school requirements, struggled through a ten-month technician's training course, and landed a job paying more than the $6.50 an hour ET clients average. . . .

Denise Richards's metamorphosis from welfare mother to working mother is fast becoming the stuff of liberal myth, the Democrats' answer to Ronald Reagan's tales of Cadillac-driving welfare queens. Republicans and Democrats have found new common ground on welfare, collaborating in state legislatures and Congress on laws to push more AFDC recipients into the labor market. . . .

These days 38 states operate programs, using a combination of carrots and sticks to lure or coerce AFDC parents into the labor market. The projects range from the voluntary, high-spending ET program in Massachusetts, to those that condition AFDC benefits on parents' seeking work or job training, to the 25 states giving some AFDC recipients "work experience" in unpaid, obligatory jobs—better known as "workfare." . . .

But while there is little doubt, least of all among the 3.6 million American adults on AFDC, that work is a better means of support than welfare for most AFDC parents, there is plenty of uncertainty about how to move them to self-support, or whether it can be done. A close look at the nation's two largest welfare-to-work experiments—Massachusetts's ET and California's Greater Avenues for Independence (GAIN)—shows that it takes more than just carrots, sticks, and even jobs to move welfare parents toward self-sufficiency.

A Successful Program

Antipoverty advocates and AFDC clients helped design ET. Technocrats run it, motivated less by ideology than bottom-line results. The state's well-organized welfare rights community constantly criticizes it. Thanks to that balancing act—and to the lowest unemployment rate in the country—ET is the nation's most successful effort at putting welfare clients to work.

Like Denise Richards, more than 70 percent of the 40,000 people who have gotten jobs since ET began in 1983 are still employed. Starting annual wages average near $13,500. Participation is voluntary, and the program still has a waiting list of AFDC clients.

As the Massachusetts program shows, the labor market—and a commitment to child-care funding—are the keys to making welfare reform work. Three percent unemployment means that previously disdained low-skill workers get new attention from employers. "A few years ago, nobody would look at our people if they didn't type 50 words a minute. Now employers come to me for students who type 30, if they have good work habits and basic skills," says Eileen Strier, job placement director for the

Joan Walsh, "Take This Job or Shove It," *Mother Jones*, September 1988. Reprinted with permission.

Somerville Center for Adult Learning Experience, an ET job training contractor.

Once parents land a job, child care helps them keep it. About half of ET's budget goes for child care, paying for care up to a year after ET clients start work (employed ET grads also keep medical coverage that first year). But the $42 million ET will spend on child care this year doesn't do much to address the availability or affordability of child care. In Boston, school-age child-care programs serve only *4 percent* of the city's school kids—nobody knows how many need care—meaning many children, like the Richards girls, go without after-school supervision even though, technically, state funds exist to pay for their care. Infant and toddler care is a "crisis," says former ET child-care administrator Ronnie Sanders.

Some Problems

Nor does the market-driven ET challenge the labor market's inequities. When a 1986 study found low wages pushed 43 percent of ET graduates back onto welfare, program officials imposed a "wage floor," requiring training contractors to place clients in jobs that pay at least $6 an hour. But most women who participate in ET are still tracked into low-wage ghettos: clerical, health, and day care jobs that keep many at near-poverty level wages. Denise Richards's annual salary of $18,600 puts her family of five about $100 a week above the poverty line. If she had to pay for child care, she'd be poorer than she was on welfare.

"Adults need a clear economic track to get interested in education."

The problems are not lost on ET contractors, who generally praise the program. At United South End Settlements, a bulwark of Boston's black community which runs ET programs, training director Cerci Kale says ET rushes job training and placement too quickly to help her more disadvantaged clients. Training, Inc. director Elsa Bengel, whose programs boast among ET's highest wage rates and job placements, puts it this way: "Most of the money flowing into job training is meant to get people off welfare, not train an undereducated population or end poverty."

In fact, skeptics on both the left and right— including almost everyone interviewed for this article, except ET officials—contend that ET's success rate comes at least partly from "creaming": serving women who would find work on their own without ET. Program administrators deny the charge, and there is no firm data one way or the other. But while ET may have begun by creaming, its current

clientele is far less job-ready than earlier volunteers. Half as many have high school diplomas or work experience. In 1988, the program is budgeted to spend $5,305 per job placement, up from $1,794 three years ago. The test of whether ET can provide a genuine alternative to welfare reliance for Massachusetts's most disadvantaged parents is only beginning.

The California Program

The jobless rate of 3.5 percent in California's Santa Clara County, the home of high-tech corridor Silicon Valley, is among the state's lowest. This is the heart of the new service economy, where the opening of the luxury Fairmont San Jose Hotel is to jobseekers what a new GM plant was a generation ago. A labor market survey conducted for GAIN, the state's welfare-reform model, lists "hospitality management" and the booming temporary-help industry as top opportunities. "Employers are concerned," according to the survey, "that many jobs paying $5, $6, $7 an hour will go unfilled."

But GAIN is off to a somewhat slow start in Santa Clara County, the first urban county in the state with the program. In its first 22 months of operation, only 866 GAIN clients out of 5,767 participants in the county left AFDC for jobs. Many more—the county has no reliable numbers—have found work, but their jobs pay so little that they are still collecting AFDC.

Across the state, counties operating GAIN—a more complicated program than ET, and mandatory for AFDC recipients with kids over six, although others may volunteer—have shown similarly lackluster job placement results. Most clients are being tracked into remedial education or English language instruction. To its credit, GAIN provides those classes to all who need them, and over two-thirds of all clients do. [In 1987], almost half of GAIN's $209 million budget went for education.

GAIN suffers from the strange alliance that built it, a collaboration between those who want to help AFDC parents toward self-support, and those who just want to cut AFDC "dependency"—and costs. The 1985 compromise, worked out by liberal San Francisco assembly member Art Agnos (who has since become the city's mayor), reflected its authors' political agendas as much as the logic of moving people toward independence. The result is a program that looks like it was designed by Rube Goldberg. Democrats built in the education mandate, for AFDC parents who lack basic skills, but the parents must finish those studies before getting job training. Republicans demanded that GAIN clients go to Job Search, where they are forced to seek jobs—and take them, if they pay more than welfare—before the state will pay for training. Democrats got child-care funds into the bill. Republicans got workfare.

In Santa Clara County, GAIN's well-intended education mandate hasn't gone over big with adults who associate school with boredom and failure, and absenteeism is high. Job training experts blame GAIN, for refusing to let clients get book learning and job training at the same time. "Adults need a clear economic track to get interested in education, and GAIN is treating people like children," says Robert Johnston of San Jose's Center for Employment Training, a GAIN contractor.

Next to education, GAIN's biggest program is Job Search. Only half the Santa Clara clients assigned there show up. Some, no doubt, are shirkers. But judging from interviews with Job Search students and graduates, many are understandably unconvinced that yet another foray into the labor market will bring them a job that will provide the benefits and wages to support a family. And many find it hard to get the job training the program was designed to provide. . . .

Child care is the single biggest obstacle to most clients' employment, says county case manager Carolyn McGee. State-funded programs in Santa Clara have waiting lists of more than 10,000 kids, and the county's efforts to extend "transitional" child care subsidies from three months after employment to a year have been refused by the state. Most GAIN parents are relying on informal care, by relatives or friends. Some leave kids alone.

And some, McGee says, are stuck in a revolving door—from GAIN out into a low-wage job that can't support a family, then back on AFDC and through GAIN again. "A woman will come to me all starry-eyed, 'Guess what, I have a job.' Then we sit down and go over her expenses, and she realizes, 'Oh well, I can't afford that.' It's hard to say, 'Let's continue on with GAIN,' because she knows she'll face the same reality six months down the road."

State officials acknowledge that most GAIN clients won't find work that pays enough to leave AFDC. Former GAIN consultant Julia Lopez thinks the program should aim to find most people "jobs that pay a decent wage. But we're never going to get *everyone* off aid. We don't have that kind of economy. Our goal should be to help people put together a household package that works. Maybe it's part work, part [AFDC] grant. There should be no shame attached to that."

Blaming Welfare

Both GAIN and (to a lesser degree) ET suffer from the Reagan-era notion that it is less important to boost poor families out of poverty than off of welfare. The welfare-to-work push represents a triumph of the antiwelfare analysis popularized by Charles Murray in his tract *Losing Ground*: that welfare itself is to blame for rising poverty, unemployment, and unmarried parenthood by providing an alternative to self-supporting work.

Murray's theories have been widely refuted. No study has ever confirmed his wild links between welfare and the social ills he blames on it, even among the 30 percent of AFDC recipients on aid eight years or more. And the strongest challenge to his work lies, ironically, in the results of the welfare-to-work experiments they have spawned.

"The welfare-to-work push represents a triumph of the antiwelfare analysis . . . that welfare itself is to blame for rising poverty."

There is little evidence that any of the commonly used welfare-to-work strategies can lead to lasting independence for most AFDC parents. Job search programs, workfare, and even most skills-training projects have had scant success in raising participants' earnings or reducing welfare reliance. San Diego's workfare experiment, the widely praised county project that led to GAIN's statewide approval, raised each participant's earnings an average of *$560 a year*. Isabel Sawhill of the Urban Institute predicts that at best, a national training effort could raise participants' earnings 3 to 6 percent, and reduce their welfare reliance 1 to 5 percent.

So what to do? The best state programs, according to an opinionated survey by attorneys Paula Roberts and Rhoda Schulzinger from the Center for Law and Social Policy, combine genuine skills training and education with job creation. They are voluntary, since it makes no sense to force parents into programs that at their best show minimal success. And they are supported by initiatives to expand child-care funding, raise the minimum wage, and extend benefits to the working poor. Maine, Massachusetts, Minnesota, and Maryland rate high in the attorneys' survey.

Young Mothers at Risk

Other antipoverty experts say programs should target the AFDC parents who will form the bulk of the long-term welfare caseload—young, never-married mothers who had their first children as teens. From Charles Murray to the Children's Defense Fund, there is consensus that those young mothers are at greatest risk for long-term welfare reliance, and that they should be the focus of education and training efforts. But neither ET nor GAIN truly targets those at-risk mothers.

ET-funded teen-parent programs, for instance, are hampered by the program's short-term focus. "These girls have so many crises in their lives, and ET won't tolerate the degree of involvement they need," says Marilyn Skipton, who directs an ET-funded program.

In California, Governor George Deukmejian wanted to cut GAIN's enormous costs by turning away volunteers, including those at-risk young mothers, in large urban counties like Los Angeles and San Francisco that aren't yet running GAIN. A compromise would allow those counties to serve a limited number of volunteers, but the plan satisfies almost no one.

Given the dismal results of welfare-to-work projects, the newest wave of antipoverty work is focusing on poor children, to give them better options than unemployment and AFDC. And children's advocates blast the current welfare reform mania for ignoring kids as it rushes mothers into the labor market. While good preschool programs, for instance, improve the school performance and life options of low-income kids, workfare programs tend to "provide the lowest-cost arrangements for the children who need the most supportive care—the same kids who are eligible for Head Start, who we design state preschool programs for," says a perplexed Helen Blank of the Children's Defense Fund.

The most perverse irony in the current welfare reform frenzy is its exclusive focus on mothers, when one of the ills it seeks to cure is the jump in families living without fathers. And the huge rise in the number of black families headed by women—from 22 percent in 1960 to 42 percent in 1983—is connected less to welfare than to the loss of jobs for black men.

From New York City to Oakland, California, blue-collar jobs once held by black men have disappeared, to be replaced by low-wage "pink-collar" positions mainly filled by women, and midlevel jobs requiring higher education. When University of Chicago scholar William Julius Wilson compared the declining numbers of nonincarcerated, employed black men per 100 black women, he found the biggest jump in female-headed households in regions with the sharpest decline in employed, "marriageable" men.

Black Employment

Feminists aren't crazy about Wilson's theory, since it seems to tie this generation of women and children to the dim prospects of black men. And it implies that there's something wrong with female-headed families, a notion black women have fought for decades. But you can't read Wilson's work—the seemingly endless data on black teen pregnancy, dropout rates and unemployment, the worsening concentration of the poor in hopeless neighborhoods, the exodus of jobs from the cities where the black poor are trapped—without knowing that the problems of poverty and isolation will only be solved by focusing on entire communities: men, women, and children.

Without a re-employment strategy for black men, transforming Denise Richards into Single Supermom,

and clubbing other welfare mothers into the work force with her, will leave us as far from a solution to poverty as we've ever been.

For all the projects' flaws, advocates and administrators of programs like ET and GAIN at least deserve some credit for taking lemons and making lemonade—they have attempted, in the current antiwelfare, antigovernment climate, to use government to make a difference in the lives of the poor. It's no small feat to have gained millions of dollars in job training and child care for welfare mothers at a time of drastic social service cuts.

Denise Richards, for one, is grateful for the help getting off welfare, even if she's far from having the kind of security and family life she wants. Burglars rewarded her for getting out of the house and into a job by breaking in and stealing the family TV set, and she worries—daily—about her girls coming home to an empty apartment in her dicey neighborhood. "I want *out* of here," she says, though she can't save enough money to plan a move anytime soon. Her income puts her out of the formal ranks of the poor, but in many ways she's still living in poverty. . . .

The best lesson of programs like ET and GAIN is that if AFDC mothers are to be expected to move from welfare to work, the state will have to fill in the gaps of today's low-wage service economy with child care and after-school programs, medical benefits, and even partial welfare grants or wage subsidies. Says GAIN architect Art Agnos: "This program is ending the debate over the worth of people on welfare. Now we're beginning to see the economic reality that's facing them."

"In a nation that shuns social planning, U.S. policymakers have long been unwilling to provide the 'social wage' entitlements common to the rest of the world."

In a nation that shuns social planning, U.S. policymakers have long been unwilling to provide the "social wage" entitlements common to the rest of the world—family allowances, subsidized child care, health care, parental leave, and job training. Now, they are backing into some of the same programs, and calling it welfare reform. But by doing it through the punitive, stigmatized AFDC system, they make sure that blame stays with parents, rather than a new economy—and outdated policies—that are increasingly failing American families.

Joan Walsh is a writer and consultant to the California State Legislature Task Force on the Changing Family.

"Social welfare programs...cannot be blamed for the increase in black female-headed families."

Welfare Helps Black Families

Kathryn Neckerman, Robert Aponte, and William Julius Wilson

Over the past two decades, explanation of the sharp rise in female-headed families among blacks has focused on the incentives that welfare programs provide. Charles Murray is the latest and perhaps the most prominent representative of this point of view. But while the welfare hypothesis was plausible in the early 1970s, following the simultaneous sharp increase in proportions of female-headed families and the unprecedented expansion of welfare, it can no longer be sustained. Sophisticated empirical research on the subject shows only modest effects of AFDC [Aid to Families with Dependent Children] on family structure. Welfare benefit levels appear to have their greatest influence not on the incidence of out-of-wedlock births or on rates of separation and divorce, but on the living arrangements of young single mothers. The experience of the past ten years confirms this research: the proportion of families headed by women has continued to rise even as the real value of welfare benefits has fallen.

Black Males and Jobs

As the welfare hypothesis had proven unfruitful, the effect of black male economic status is again receiving attention. In historical and ethnographic studies as well as in multivariate analyses of survey data, male economic status is consistently related to family stability. Research indicates that increasing black male joblessness, in combination with the high mortality and incarceration rates of black men, has resulted in dramatic declines over the past twenty-five years in the ratio of employed men to women, or the "male marriageable pool index [MMPI]." Not only are national trends consistent with the hypothesis that male joblessness is related to the rise

of female-headed households, but also, when these data are disaggregated by region, they show that in regions where the black MMPI fell the most—the Northeast and Midwest—the proportion of black female-headed families also increased the most. The more modest increase in families headed by women among whites is accompanied by little change in white MMPI values.

Economic shifts are likely to be a major factor in the increasing joblessness of black men. Regional differences in the change in MMPI discussed earlier point to the particular importance of industrial transformations occurring in the Northeast and Midwest. The shift from manufacturing to services and the geographic shifts in production activity have altered both the number and the characteristics of jobs available in areas where blacks are concentrated. Most inner-city blacks cannot qualify for high-skilled positions in the finance, real estate, and information-processing sectors; low-skilled service jobs, however, are characterized by low wages, restricted opportunities for advancement, and unstable employment.

A Sensitive Subject

Despite the consistent evidence linking male economic status to family stability, until recently most scholars and policymakers have overlooked joblessness in their discussions of changing family structure. Because official unemployment statistics do not take into account discouraged workers, or those who have dropped out of the labor force, they understate the increase in black male joblessness; thus it is possible that the extent of the problem has escaped the notice of social scientists concerned with the black family. A more likely explanation, however, lies in the sensitive and highly politicized nature of the debate over the black family. Although previous historical and ethnographic accounts had

Kathryn Neckerman, Robert Aponte, and William Julius Wilson, "Family Structure, Black Unemployment, and American Social Policy." Margaret Weir, et al. *The Politics of Social Policy in the United States.* Copyright © 1988 by Princeton University Press. Excerpt, pp. 414-419, reprinted with permission of Princeton University Press.

often portrayed the lower-class black family as unstable or disorganized, Daniel Patrick Moynihan's *The Negro Family* generated a tremendous amount of controversy, and this criticism had a chilling effect on research on the black family. Most scholarly writing that addressed the subject at all emphasized the resilience and adaptability of lower-class black families in the face of overwhelming disadvantage. Ironically, this focus had led to a neglect of traditional liberal concerns, such as problems of racial isolation and restricted economic opportunity and the impact of these problems on the family, even as the economic and demographic shifts of the 1970s have made these concerns increasingly timely. Conservative scholars, who were not inhibited by this ideologically tinged criticism, came to dominate the debate with their arguments of welfare dependency and the culture of poverty.

"No government . . . can avoid having policies that profoundly influence family relationships."

Research agendas on the family must be broadened to take account of macrostructural forces such as employment trends. Although we have evidence that male economic status is related to family stability, much work remains to be done. Still unresolved is the role of factors such as ethnicity, class, and community in mediating the influence of male unemployment on marriage and family relations. Those concerned with contemporary family problems may be able to draw on the insights of a rich and growing literature in history of the family.

Even as this research proceeds, however, we must develop new policy approaches to female-headed families and the related problems of welfare dependency and teenage childbearing. Although the liberal social welfare programs of the 1960s cannot be blamed for the increase in black female-headed families, they also have been helpless to stop it. Further, these Great Society programs have shown only limited success in alleviating the poverty of female-headed families; even when poverty rates are adjusted for receipt of non-cash benefits, one-fourth of all female-headed families are still poor.

Comprehensive Reform

One major component of a policy approach to the problems of female-headed families must be a comprehensive economic reform package designed to promote and enhance employment among the disadvantaged—both men and women. Fundamental to this approach are policies that will foster economic growth and create a tight labor market.

The logic of supply and demand indicates that policies to create a tight labor market may also raise wages; historically, in addition, other employer concessions such as company-sponsored day care have also been provided when labor is scarce. However, without protectionist legislation or measures such as employee ownership/control, unskilled or semiskilled workers, especially those in production, are vulnerable to the same economic shifts now devastating the older industrial cities. Low-skilled workers who are paid well enough to escape poverty are for that very reason likely to lose their jobs, either to mechanization or to international competition. To address the problem of joblessness, we need macroeconomic and labor market policies sophisticated enough to come to terms with this dilemma.

This problem points as well to the importance of measures such as adult education, on-the-job training, and apprenticeship to raise the skill levels of the disadvantaged. Wide disparities in education and training perpetuate inequality in the American labor force and represent a formidable obstacle to anti-poverty efforts. Lack of skills also leaves workers vulnerable to fluctuations in economic conditions and to future technological change. Improved manpower policies would ensure that the disadvantaged are not permanently trapped on the lowest rungs of the job market.

Employment Is Not Enough

Employment policies are not typically seen as an answer to the problems of female-headed families. Research shows that a rising tide does not raise all boats equally: Economic growth helps male-headed families more than female-headed families. Our work suggests that these employment policies will address the problems of female-headed families indirectly, by improving the job prospects of men and enhancing the stability of low-income two-parent families. But even under our current set of social policies, economic growth improves the economic status of women who head families, and it will do so more effectively with policy efforts to improve child care services and child support enforcement. The majority of women heading families are in the labor force, and more can be drawn in by more attractive job prospects and better child care. In addition, in combination with better child support enforcement, economic growth helps custodial parents, mostly women, by raising the earnings of absent parents.

In the foreseeable future, however, employment by itself may not raise a family, whether single-parent or two-parent, out of poverty. Many families will still need income support. Therefore, these economic policies must be supplemented with a program of welfare reform and related measures to address the problems of the current income transfer system: inadequate levels of support, cross-state inequities, work disincentives, and lack of provisions for poor two-parent families. At the very minimum, a national AFDC benefit standard, adjusted each year for inflation, is certainly needed. Income support for single-parent families might take the form of the Child Support Assurance Program, developed by Irwin Garfinkel and currently underway on a demonstration basis in Wisconsin. Under this program, a minimum benefit per child is guaranteed to single-parent families regardless of the income of the custodial parent. The absent parent's earnings are taxed at a fixed rate, and if the resulting payment is less than the minimum benefit, the state contributes the rest out of general revenues. This program provides a more adequate level of income support—less stigmatized, with no work disincentives, but with little or no additional cost to the state.

Influencing Families

Some Western European countries provide support through family or child allowances. Moynihan has noted that tax expenditures through the Earned Income Tax Credit and standard deductions are a form of child allowance already available to American families—one that has been severely eroded by inflation, but one in place nevertheless. It may be easier to make incremental changes in this arrangement than to institute an entirely new program. Even more important than Moynihan's specific policy recommendations, however, may be this reminder that "no government, however firm might be its wish otherwise, can avoid having policies that profoundly influence family relationships. This is not to be avoided. The only option is whether these will be purposeful, intended policies or whether they will be residual, derivative, in a sense concealed ones."

"Failure to address racial differences in family structure will ... lead to neglect of the plight of the black urban underclass."

These policies are likely to enjoy more widespread political support than the set of means-tested programs presently targeted at the poor. "Universal programs," those available to working- and middle-class segments of society as well as to the poor, are more likely to attract political support, and therefore more generous and stable funding, because all classes have a stake in them. Means-tested programs, on the other hand, are associated with a low-income and minority constituency, and thus they are not programs that most voters identify with. Economic growth and tight labor market policies, child allowances, and child support enforcement are

programs that all segments of society might participate in or benefit from, even though the most disadvantaged groups (such as the ghetto underclass) would reap disproportionate benefits.

Racial Differences

An emphasis on universal programs to attack problems in the black community that historically have been related to racial subjugation represents a fundamental shift from the traditional approach of addressing problems associated with race. It is true, as we have tried to show in this paper, that the growth in the proportions of families headed by women, and the related problems of poverty, long-term welfare dependency, and teenage out-of-wedlock childbearing, are for historical reasons concentrated in the black community. And, as we have also noted, failure to address racial differences in family structure will distort the debate over changes in family structure and lead to neglect of the plight of the black urban underclass. However, to stress the prevalence of these problems among blacks does not mean that race-specific policies are the only or the most effective way to address them. Indeed, race-specific policies such as affirmative action traditionally have aided the most advantaged members of the minority population, have difficulty attracting widespread popular support, and have failed to address the fundamental source of recent black family disintegation—the economic shifts have fallen most heavily on the truly disadvantaged segment of the black community. America's future challenge in social policy, therefore, is to improve the life chances of groups such as the ghetto underclass by emphasizing programs to which the more advantaged groups of all races can positively relate.

The authors are associated with the Urban Family Life Project, a study being conducted by the University of Chicago's Department of Sociology.

"The government simply must stop subsidizing the failure of family formation."

Welfare Undermines Black Families

William Tucker

Perhaps no problem poses a greater danger to the future of American society than the emergence of a seemingly permanent "underclass" built around the single-parent, female-headed household. Previous generations of Americans have known poverty, but to none did it seem so hopeless. All saw America as a land of opportunity, and even among the poor there was a strong sense that hard work and long-term effort would pay off—which, with astonishing regularity, it did. The experience of recent immigrant groups, most notably Asians, proves that the system still works. But among today's underclass, particularly among American blacks, efforts at improvement seem to lead backwards. For the underclass, things are actually worse now than they were twenty-five years ago, when the most concentrated attempts in our history to remove institutional racism began.

The litany of problems in black, lower-class communities needs no introduction. Half of all black children are now being raised in single-parent homes—up from 20 percent in 1960. Almost 60 percent of black babies are born illegitimate. These "welfare families" form a solid core of poverty around which a tangle of pathologies cluster. . . .

Over the brief period 1967-1970—as the civil rights revolution crested and the economy neared full employment—the national percentage of eligible single black mothers on welfare zoomed from 62 to 91 percent. Welfare rolls burgeoned from 4.4 million in 1965 to 9.7 million in 1970 and the percentage of female-headed households among blacks rose from 24 percent to 31 percent. With no relation whatsoever to the nearly full-employment economy, the "welfare culture" of single-parent households quickly became the norm in low-income black communities. Almost by accident, the small widows-and-orphans pension of the New Deal had become America's family policy.

Married to the Government

For a while America did have another kind of family policy, through the income-tax deduction. As economist Eugene Steuerle pointed out in *Taxing the Family*, as late as 1948 a family with four children making the median income of $3,187 was completely exempted from taxes by the $600 deduction for dependents. Inflation has since devoured these benefits. From 1960 to 1984, single people faced an essentially flat tax rate, while couples with two children saw their taxes rise 43 percent and couples with four children a remarkable 223 percent.

The poor have thus become caught in a pincer movement. Regulation of the labor market, which assured the prosperity of the middle class, has limited the ability of the poor to work their way out of poverty. Meanwhile, AFDC [Aid to Families with Dependent Children] has offered poor *women* an alternative occupation: single motherhood. As Mikhail Bernstam and Peter Swan of the Hoover Institution put it, the government has become "the marriage partner of last resort"—maybe even of first resort, since almost 90 percent of black teenage mothers no longer marry. . . .

The reasons for the collapse of black culture, then, are fairly clear. The big question is, does anybody really care to do anything about it? . . .

Democrats continue to try to gather everyone under one tent. When the system reaches its natural limits, they shout, "Full employment!" and watch the inflationary fires burn. Republicans, for their part, preach supply-side economics—which has dramatically reduced unemployment, but still seems incapable of picking up the most unemployable. When this system reaches its limits, Republicans ask

William Tucker, "Our Homestead Plan for the Poor," *The American Spectator*, July 1988. Reprinted with permission.

churches to make up the difference, or pretend the problems don't exist.

As a compromise, both parties seem to have settled on something called "workfare." . . .

Ersatz Independence

Although nobody wants to admit it, the new "workfare" system is essentially going to look like this:

(1) Female teenagers will qualify for the program by getting pregnant. This will make them eligible for job-training and other educational benefits.

(2) Under the direction of the state, they will undergo intensive educational efforts to teach them to function fairly independently.

(3) If all goes well, they will be turned back to society within a few years—as capable as possible of raising their children without the help of men.

Thus, if workfare is *successful*, the single-parent, female-headed household will become institutionalized even beyond the incentives of AFDC. Any question of whether poor black men can break back into this family structure is essentially moot. The system has given up on them and is concentrating on those who *may* still make it: black women.

Is there any alternative to this Rube Goldberg system that virtually begs women to become pregnant and then uses this failure as an opportunity to teach them ersatz independence? I propose there is.

The first thing we must do is take a holistic approach—look at the entire life cycle of a member of the underclass and ask ourselves where the intervention of the state can be expected to do the most good. After all, the entire present system has been improvised out of fifty years of backing and filling—patching up a system that was wrongly conceived in the first place.

In 1984, Leon Dash, a veteran *Washington Post* investigator, spent a year living in a welfare-dependent housing project that has the highest rate of illegitimacy in Washington, fully one out of four children being born to unwed teenagers. Before moving in, Dash said, he had been given several interpretations of teenage pregnancies. Conservatives told him girls had babies just to collect welfare grants. Liberals said teenage births came because girls were ignorant of birth-control or were leading dreary lives and wanted someone to love. "Neither prediction turned out to be true," Dash noted.

Instead, he found a world where, for boys and girls alike, having a child has become a "rite of passage." Young people simply cannot imagine an adult life beyond age 19 or so. They are grown-ups at 12, want children as quickly as possible (in order to prove their man- or womanhood), and place enormous peer pressure on any "goody two-shoes" who is not sexually active or pregnant by age 15. . . .

What can the larger society offer in such a situation? Certainly, some kind of financial assistance is essential. But how can such assistance encourage positive goals rather than reward failure?

I suggest that we should revive—metaphorically, at least—what was perhaps America's most successful effort to even the scales between rich and poor: the Homestead program. After 1862, the government made land grants available out of the public lands. The program continued until 1916. Altogether, 80 million acres were granted to 500,000 claimants. Certainly, not all deserving people got land; probably a lot of undeserving people got what they shouldn't have. But the program worked. The "safety valve" of the Homestead program is often credited with preventing the development of a permanently impoverished underclass in the nineteenth century.

"The whole point would be to give teenagers something to look forward to, *an organizing principle around which to control their present behavior."*

Such vast expanses of public land, of course, are no longer available. But the *principle* of the Homestead program could be made the basis of a policy that would give impoverished youth the "hand up" in their effort to become productive members of society. Beginning in some specific year—1990, for instance—every young person who has lived below the poverty line for three years should be given a $5,000 cash grant when they reach age 21. The grant would replace AFDC. Anyone on AFDC in 1990 could remain on the rolls so long as they were eligible—or they could "cash in" their benefits for a similar one-time $5,000 grant. But no new cases would be opened. AFDC as we now know it would thus be phased out over the next generation and return to being a program *only* for widows and orphans.

What would such a "New Homestead Program" cost? It's easy to calculate. There are 35 million people currently living below the poverty line. Of those, about one in twenty-two—1.5 million—turn 21 each year. The annual cost would thus be $7.5 billion—half of what AFDC costs today. Another option could be to allow individuals to "bank" their grants and receive $10,000 each at age 25, when they could put it to even better use. A husband and wife, each with a $10,000 grant, could make a down payment on half the homes sold in this country.

Welfare and Fertility

The first principle of such a system, of course, would be to cut the link between welfare benefits and fertility. The government simply must stop subsidizing the failure of family formation. Even more important, however, the "New Homestead Program" would give poor teenagers a reasonable chance of getting a start at the age when they *should* be taking their first steps toward independence. A homestead grant would give them something to look forward to in life—and also distribute benefits more equitably between the sexes.

Some reformers would probably want to attach all kinds of conditions to the grant—you must graduate from high school, you must have a job, you cannot have illegitimate children. But I believe there must be some assumption of responsibility. If people blow the whole $5,000 on drugs or clothes, that's their problem. But afterwards they must realize that, as able-bodied citizens, they're on their own. No more marrying the government, no more chronic dependency, no more living off state subsidies for anti-social, anti-familial behavior.

An Incentive

The whole point would be to *give teenagers something to look forward to*, an organizing principle around which to control their present behavior. When philanthropist Eugene Lang promised a class of Harlem sixth-graders that he would pay for their college education if they finished high school, nearly all of them did just that. That's the kind of principle we should be pursuing.

Paul Weyrich, of the Free Congress Foundation, has proposed a pact between conservatives and minority leaders over welfare reform. He suggests that conservatives promise to support any program, *no matter what it costs*, as long as it takes the negative incentives out of welfare and promises to set low-income blacks and others on a permanent path to family stability and independent functioning.

Perhaps the most important thing to remember is that the old verities do work. Family, community, initiative, self-reliance—the traditional qualities that made America—have not been defeated by the twentieth century. They have merely been overshadowed for a while by the collectivist fantasies that have mesmerized the intelligentsia—and, to some extent, the public as well.

William Tucker is the New York correspondent of The American Spectator *magazine.*

"The U.S. economy, despite all its creaks and groans, continues to be a miraculous...success."

America's Economy Is Strong

Warren T. Brookes

On May 26, 1988, the Commerce Department revised its first quarter GNP [gross national product] growth estimate from 2.3 to 3.9 percent, from solid growth to a powerful surge. Yet the media treated this good news as a "new threat to inflation." The same pundits who were warning the nation of a recession or a depression now are warning us either of "the dangers of a boom," or of the economy's impending takeover by foreign powers.

There was a cartoon in the *Christian Science Monitor*—a normally moderate and sensible organ—showing Uncle Sam as a bedraggled and grease-stained mechanic standing next to the open hood of a tattered, over-sized, broken-down American car, labeled "U.S. economy." He was eyeing an on-rushing Model-T filled with Hispanics labeled "Latin American Debtors," all of them yelling cheerily at Uncle Sam, "Going our way?" The implication was clear: the *Monitor*, like the rest of the establishment press, tends to see the U.S. economy as a banana republic headed down the Latin American route, laden with external debt, ready to default at any moment.

A Sick Economy?

But, just a week or so before that cartoon appeared, Charles Wolf and Sarah Hooker of the Rand Corporation reported in the *Wall Street Journal* that when our foreign investments are properly valued at market level, the U.S. in 1986 was a net *creditor* nation, to the tune of at least $50 billion—instead of $264 billion in debt, as the Commerce Department reported.

The reason for this is that the "net debt" position reported by Commerce is based on valuing all investments at book, not market, value. Since most of the U.S. investment abroad was made ten to thirty

years ago, it is badly undervalued, while virtually all of the foreign investment in the U.S. was made in the last decade, and is closer to its real market value.

Not a Debtor Nation

Rand's common sense analysis was backed up by a simple fact: In 1986, when we supposedly became "the largest debtor nation on earth," U.S. income from overseas investments was $20.8 billion greater than U.S. payments to foreign creditors and investors. As Milton Friedman politely told the Commerce Department in an article, "If your income from investments exceeds the cost of carrying your investments, you are clearly *not* a debtor."

The point of these examples should be clear. Shallow economic reporting and a fountain of misinformation have combined to spook and depreciate an otherwise booming economy.

That economy is now in . . . a peacetime recovery whose *average* GNP growth has been nearly 4 percent a year, and which has created over 15 million jobs even as it cut inflation from 12.6 percent to less than 4 percent, and put on the best competitiveness performance in the postwar history of the United States. In the process it has destroyed the ugly Phillips Curve, which postulated that there was a trade-off between inflation and unemployment.

That's the *good* news.

The *bad* news is that few Americans, and even very few investors, seem to know the good news. . . .

The greatest irony of the Reagan recovery is that its loudest noise was made on October 19 of 1987. Yet at the moment of the market crash, the U.S. economy was expanding at its most rapid rate since 1983, with industrial production up over 5 percent, total jobs up over 3 million, and manufacturing jobs

Warren T. Brookes, "The Silent Boom," *The American Spectator*, August 1988. Reprinted with permission.

then up 340,000 from the year before—a rate of growth that expanded to 466,000 a year as of April 1988.

Factory capacity was at peak operating levels, as was the employment ratio, along with help-wanted advertising, and consumer confidence. Capital spending was surging at the fastest rate in three years, manufacturing profit reports were the highest since the 1960s, and exports were soaring by 20 percent, in an economy where unit sales per worker were rising more than thirteen percentage points faster than unit labor costs. . . .

The Plain Truth

If an ignorant alien were to visit the U.S. today and simply listen to the network news or read the *Washington Post* (whose stories are regurgitated by the press around the country), they would think the country is on the brink of depression. . . .

The plain truth is that the current recovery . . . has been stronger than any peacetime recovery in our history, with GNP growth and per capita income growth setting a far stronger pace than anyone has noticed. (See Table 1.)

One reason this recovery has been so "silent" is that it has been fueled not by the big noisy corporations, but by an entrepreneurial boom in smaller businesses. As Joel Kotkin, the west coast editor of *INC.* magazine, put it in an article in the January 17, 1988 *Washington Post*, "From Thatcher's England to Takeshita's Japan, emulating America's entrepreneurial explosion has become a fundamental goal of policy-makers. . . . While large corporations lost 1.4 million manufacturing jobs between 1974 and 1984, those losses were virtually made up by positions created by 41,000 *new* industrial companies formed during that period. Companies with fewer than 250 employees, which now make up some 42 percent of all manufacturing employment, could constitute an absolute majority by the early 1990's."

As Peter Drucker puts it, "America shares equally in the crisis that afflicts all developed countries, but in entrepreneurship, in creating the different and the new, the U.S. is way out in front." Indeed, since 1982, U.S. industrial production has almost silently risen over 26 percent, compared with Japan's 22 percent, West Germany's 11.6 percent, and Europe's 8.8 percent. . . .

Over the last seven years we have been told one lie about the U.S. economy after another.

Take, for example, the myth about the nation's supposedly declining savings rate, as simplistically measured by the Commerce Department, and our supposedly soaring debt burden. While our debt has indeed risen dramatically, even counting the crash, our financial wealth has (quietly) risen even faster, making us more solvent than ever before.

It may come as a surprise to discover that in 1986, U.S. financial wealth, as measured by the Federal

Reserve "Flow of Funds" analysis, reached 244 percent of GNP—an all-time high, and up hugely from the 181.4 percent level of 1981. Even after the crash that figure remains over 240 percent.

Indeed, since 1980, U.S. financial wealth in constant 1982 dollars has soared 53.3 percent. In the 1970s that number rose only 17.6 percent. So the rise in the U.S. financial wealth under the Reagan Administration at over 7 percent a year, real, has been nearly five times the average 1.6 percent a year in the 1970s.

Table 1

Economic Growth Trends
in Two 5-Year Periods

	1975-80	1982-87
Real GNP Growth		
Total	% 18.3	% 19.8
Per Year	3.4	3.7
Real Disposable Income		
Total	% 14.6	% 18.3
Per Capita	8.7	12.9
Annual p/c	1.7	2.5

Source: U.S. Commerce Department
Bureau of Economic Analysis

But what about our vast new debt to the rest of the world? Aside from the incredible overstatement of that "debt," most of it represents ready and willing investment in U.S. assets (property, factories, stocks, bonds, deposits in U.S. banks for factoring purposes) because the U.S. is now the world's hottest economy. Or as Joel Kotkin put it in the *Post*: "In fact, periods of heaviest foreign investment usually coincided with the most dynamic U.S. expansions, particularly in the late 19th and early 20th centuries when American industrial prowess overcame that of all European competitors. After several decades of American capital flight to other parts of the world, the same process is now repeating itself. Faced with declining populations, high unemployment and anemic economic growth, European investors again consider the U.S. a good place to put their money." It may shock you to know that right now overseas investors hold less than 5 percent of U.S. financial assets.

Ironically, the single most important reason we are now a "debtor nation" (and have a big trade deficit) was the 1982 decision by U.S. banks to stop throwing good money after bad and reduce foreign lending from $110 billion a year to less than $2 billion in 1985. This alone, and not the influx of new credit, turned our "net creditor" position into the current net "debtor" position. And it was this sudden sharp shift from creditor to debtor that was the main stimulus for exploding the trade deficit.

In January 1988 President Reagan told a Cleveland audience that "trade deficits and inflows of foreign capital are not necessarily a sign of an economy's weakness. They are more often a sign of strength." This immediately caused stifled smirks on the part of the know-nothing network newsfolk. CBS's Jacqueline Adams told her viewers, "Of course few economists or investors agree with that view." In fact there are virtually no serious economists, left to right, who *don't* agree with it. The last time we had a merchandise trade surplus was in 1975, when unemployment was over 9 percent—and the last time our current account was in surplus was in the 1980-81 recessions.

US Competitiveness

All of which explodes still another myth—namely the supposed decline in U.S. competitiveness. In 1987, Britain's prestigious National Institute of Economic and Social Research published a study showing that the U.S. now has the most competitive labor costs in the world.

This, more than the falling dollar, explains why U.S. exports are soaring (merchandise exports alone are rising at a 30 percent rate), and why our manufacturing production is now rising at a humongous 6.4 percent annual rate—the fastest of the major industrial nations—while Japan is now importing its own cars from the U.S.

Yet in April 1988 former president Jimmy Carter was allowed to get away with holding a national seminar in Atlanta, Georgia, on the subject of "restoring U.S. competitiveness." At the moment the conference began the U.S. was registering the sixty-sixth month of the greatest rise in industrial competitiveness of any period since World War II, as the Labor Department reported that manufacturing productivity rose by a solid 2.9 percent annual rate in the first quarter of 1988—buttressed by a stunning 33 percent annualized rise in capital spending on new plant and equipment.

At the same time, unit labor costs—the key ingredient in our world competitiveness—actually *fell* at a one percent annual rate, following a nearly 2 percent fall for all of 1987.

This means that as of mid-1988, U.S. productivity stands 29 percent higher than in 1981, when President Carter left office, for an average annual rise of 4.2 percent a year—the greatest and most prolonged rise in U.S. history.

At the same time, unit labor costs in manufacturing stand nearly one percent *lower* than in 1981. This is the most stunning reduction in relative labor costs for any nation in the last twenty years, except Japan—and even Japan has barely matched our own performance since 1982. And when you factor in the 40 percent drop in the dollar's relative exchange rate against our biggest competitors, the improvement is even more remarkable. As Irwin Jacobs, chairman of

MINSTAR, said on "Wall Street Week": "This country has never been better postured from an industrial side to flourish."

Labor Shortages

Ironically, as a result of our soaring competitiveness, and our sudden export boom, the greatest danger facing the country today is not "exporting jobs," as the political myth goes, but increasing labor shortages. Since 1982, our employment has grown three times as fast as Japan's and ten times as fast as Europe's. . . .

Of all the lies about the Reagan recovery, none has been more egregious than the Democrats' charge that most of the 15 million new jobs have been for "hamburger flippers." . . .

In fact, the Labor Department reports that 63 percent of all new jobs were "Managerial and Professional," its highest paying and skills category, while only one percent were in "service occupations." . . .

"This country has never been better postured from an industrial side to flourish."

But the best proof that the low-paying jobs thesis was bunkum came when the Census Bureau's report on family income and poverty showed not only a 4.2 percent rise in median family income in 1986 (the largest rise since 1972), but also that since 1981 median family income in real dollars had risen by 9.1 percent. (In the Carter budget years 1977-81, it *fell* by 6.8 percent!) . . .

Critics scoffed at President Reagan's 1988 State of the Union contention that the American dream has been restored—but the Census income data clearly bear him out. They show that the main reason why incomes are rising again is that *all* groups are "trading up" to higher incomes, after "trading down" during the late 1970s.

From 1977-81, the percentage of families with incomes under $12,500 (constant 1986 dollars) *rose* from 34.7 percent to 36.6 percent for blacks, and from 13.9 to 15.9 percent for whites. But, since 1981, that picture was reversed, as the low-income percentage for blacks *fell* from 36.6 percent to 33.5 percent, and for whites back to 14.7 percent.

At the same time, even as these families were moving back to the middle class, the middle class itself was losing even larger numbers to the upper-income brackets above $50,000. From 1981 to 1986, the share of white families with incomes over $50,000 shot up from 16.6 percent to 22.0 percent, a huge 33 percent rise—offsetting a 7 percent drop from 1977-81.

But the most striking progress was made by blacks, whose share of families over $50,000 rose from 7.1 percent to 12 percent, an impressive 69 percent rise, after a 12.3 percent loss during 1977-81. What is happening, then, is that even as the low incomes are moving up, the middle is "vanishing" upwards.

The Final Myth

Which brings us to the final myth, perpetrated by the otherwise sensible *Economist*, namely that our "faltering growth in the standard of living is not the stuff dreams are made on, certainly not the American Dream."

Yet an analysis by the Organization for Economic Cooperation and Development (OECD) shows that "living standards in the U.S. continue to soar well above those of other Western countries." Using what they call "purchasing power parities" (PPP), OECD found that not only is U.S. real per capita GNP 10 percent ahead of its nearest competitor (Canada), it is 41 percent ahead of Japan, 33 percent ahead of West Germany, and 51 percent ahead of Great Britain, a clear proof that we remain competitive, with real U.S. PPP income rising another 4.3 percent in 1986 over 1985.

"The U.S. has created nearly 90 percent of all the new jobs in the Western world since 1980."

All in all, when you consider that the U.S. has created nearly 90 percent of all the new jobs in the Western world since 1980, this upward income performance in an era of exploding competition has been nothing short of incredible—and another testament to the fact that the U.S. economy, despite all its creaks and groans, continues to be a miraculous (if awfully quiet) success, and especially over the last five years when it has consistently outdone the world on every other indicator possible.

Warren T. Brookes is a nationally syndicated columnist for the Detroit News.

"The United States is becoming a second rate economic power."

viewpoint 13

America's Economy Is Weak

Financial Forecaster

Forbes magazine says: "We are living in an era that can truly be called revolutionary. An era where economic changes are causing far reaching political and social shifts in the world. Just one single consequence: The United States' four-decade-old domination of the world economy is coming to an end."

Forbes is right. The United States is becoming a second rate economic power.

You may not like to hear that the United States is losing its premier place in the world. But that is exactly what the facts show.

According to Lester Thurow, economist and Dean of MIT's [Massachusetts Institute of Technology] Sloan School of Management, "After World War II, the U.S. had 50 percent of the world GNP [gross national product] and could play locomotive for the world whenever growth slowed. Now the U.S. is down to 23 percent of the world GNP and can't play locomotive."

The fact is, our country is no longer an isolated economic giant.

It's as though America woke up one morning and found Japanese producers only a few miles off our Pacific coast, German industry a stone's throw off our Atlantic shore, and low-cost Far East manufacturers—which didn't even exist a few years ago—setting up shop right down the road.

Australia, New Zealand and many South American countries are producing more farm products than ever before and are pushing down the prices of our agricultural output.

Foreigners are now major investors in our financial markets, and have become major buyers of U.S. real estate and U.S. businesses.

On a large scale—looking at the American economy as a whole—things don't seem so bad. In fact, many of the statistics paint a bright picture of America in the '80s.

• [The] unemployment rate has fallen to about 5.8% from 10.7% in 1982.

• Inflation is down to between 4% and 5% (as measured by the government's Consumer Price Index).

• And the longest peacetime economic expansion on record is still intact.

On the surface, these statistics look pretty good.

But if we look at what's happening to *individuals*, rather than at the government's economic numbers, we see a much gloomier picture.

Trouble for Average Americans

Average Americans—and even many wealthy Americans—are in trouble today. And to a large extent, the reason for this trouble is the internationalization of our economy. As the world economy has grown, the U.S. economy has suffered.

Why? In simple terms, because American producers and workers must now compete with foreign producers and workers who earn far smaller profits and wages. Here are the grim statistics:

The real earnings of American workers rose steadily for 25 straight years—from 1947 to 1972. But that was the peak. Since 1972, real wages have been in a 16-year tailspin! *That's right, a 16-year decline.*

By 1986, average weekly earnings (adjusted for inflation) were 14% *below* their 1972 highs!

Putting all figures in inflation-adjusted 1977 dollars—in order to make the comparisons fair—the average weekly earnings of non-farm workers fell from a high of $198.41 in 1972 to $171.07 in 1986.

In the meantime, the average mortgage payment on new housing just passed $1,000. Is it any wonder then, that fewer Americans can afford to own a new

Financial Forecaster, "The U.S. Economy . . . and Your Financial Future Are at Greater Risk than at Any Time in History," April 1988. Reprinted with permission.

house? Or that the typical American family now needs *two* wage earners just to stay even?

The government's unemployment rate may be lower than it was six years ago. But based on average earnings, *the typical American worker is worse off today than he was 16 years ago.*

How can people be worse off if unemployment is down? One reason is that unemployment is not *really* down. Unemployment is low *only* if it is compared to 1982—the worst recession year since the Great Depression of the 1930s. In other words, the government can only say that unemployment is low if it compares today's unemployment rate with the rate that existed during the last recession. Based on historical standards, unemployment is still very high.

Competing with Foreign Labor

The most important reason for the declining standard of living is that American workers are now being forced to compete with workers in China, Korea, Yugoslavia, Poland and every other country.

Here's how it works. If Koreans can manufacture cars using labor that costs only a few dollars per hour and sell those cars in the United States, they can undercut the prices of U.S. manufacturers that pay union workers close to $25 per hour.

As a result, U.S. producers sell fewer cars. And the fewer cars U.S. manufacturers sell, the greater the downward pressure is on the wages of U.S. auto workers.

A few years ago, countries such as Korea did not have the technology, the business know-how, the capital, or the organization to produce automobiles for the U.S. market. But they do now. And even if these countries don't seem to be shipping a huge number of cars to the United States, many of them are sending parts that are used by American manufacturers to produce "American" cars. As a result, the real wages of U.S. workers have been declining for the past 16 years.

What happened 16 years ago to set off such a decline? One thing was the Arab oil embargo that turned the U.S. economy upside down. Another was that the Japanese began to seriously export automobiles to America. In other words, 16 years ago we began to import foreign goods on a larger scale than ever before.

The world is modernizing. And that means that American manufacturers are being forced to compete with producers in virtually every country in the world. Even industries that used to be "sacred" to America are no longer safe. Other countries are catching up fast and passing us in many areas.

No longer are countries such as Japan, Korea or Taiwan sending us the cheap toys you probably remember from the 1950s and 1960s. These countries are now shipping us top quality goods— from electronics to automobiles. Today, "Made in

Japan" means quality, not junk. And in many cases it means *better* quality than "Made in the USA."

There is an even more alarming way that U.S. workers are being thrown into competition with low-wage workers in other countries. That's by having U.S. corporations move their production to countries with cheap labor . . . or by purchasing manufactured parts from these countries.

The following table lists the seven largest public manufacturing companies in America, and gives the percentage of total workers employed by each company *outside* the United States. As you can see, the numbers are startling.

Corporation	Employed Outside the United States
IBM	40%
Exxon	54%
General Electric	20%
General Motors	40%
DuPont	21%
Philip Morris	38%
Coca-Cola	56%

Are these corporations wrong to look abroad to maximize their profits? That's a difficult question to answer. But the issue is not whether they "should" do it; the fact is that they *are* doing it. And the result is that American workers are being replaced by lower-priced foreign labor.

But direct competition with foreign producers is just one reason for the decline in American living standards.

What our research has uncovered is that virtually every economic problem we are now facing can be traced to the international economy. In other words, the decline in our living standards is no longer a domestic issue.

Any list of the most crucial economic problems facing America today would have to include the following seven issues:

1. Slow economic growth
2. U.S. bank failures
3. High interest rates
4. The $2.5 trillion national debt
5. The annual budget deficits
6. The possibility of a recession
7. The likelihood of escalating inflation

In the past these would have been considered "domestic" problems. Today, each one is an international issue.

Problem One
Slow Economic Growth

The current economic recovery is praised by the administration in Washington. But even the

President knows that the waning expansion is not strong enough to create true prosperity.

- Banks are failing at the alarming rate of almost 200 per year.
- Real earnings of U.S. workers are declining.
- And the percentage of Americans that can afford to be homeowners is shrinking.

In the past we would have turned to domestic policies to get the economy going. Instead, the administration is now asking Japan and West Germany to boost *their* economies so that *their* consumers will buy more of our products.

For the first time in history we are looking to other nations to solve *our* domestic problems for us.

Unfortunately, economic growth has been slowing worldwide. According to *The New York Times*, the global economy grew by about 5% per year during the 1950s and 1960s. In the 1970s, world growth slowed to about 3% per year. In the 1980s, growth slid to about 2.3% per year. And the outlook for the next few years is for a continued slide.

In other words, the "good old days" really *were* good. Living standards actually improved dramatically in the 1950s and 1960s. But no longer.

And now that American workers must compete with workers in other countries, American living standards are being dragged down to the levels of foreign workers.

Problem Two

U.S. Bank Failures

Banks are failing for one reason—bad loans.

And a majority of these bad loans can be explained by changes in the world economy. Some of the bad loans were made to Third World countries that cannot repay them. Others were made to Americans who can't repay them because of changes in the international economy.

U.S. agriculture is suffering because foreigners slashed their purchases of our products and because foreign agriculture is expanding. In fact, for the first time ever the U.S. is importing more produce than it is exporting!

And as we've all seen, falling oil prices have destroyed business and real estate values in large sectors of the U.S. economy.

The result of these changes has been an enormous number of personal and business bankruptcies . . . and the writing off of billions of dollars in bank loans.

Problem Three

High Interest Rates

Because of our huge trade deficits, the United States must attract roughly $150 billion a year from overseas to help finance our meager economic recovery. And in order to attract all this foreign capital we have to keep interest rates high.

However, high interest rates raise mortgage payments, making it more difficult to afford a house.

High interest rates raise the cost of borrowing, making it more difficult for consumers to buy on credit.

And high interest rates raise the cost of capital to business, which slows investment in new plants and equipment and drags down the rate of economic growth.

As a result, your home is costing you more than it should. And your income is probably growing much slower than it should!

Also, a large part of foreign investment is in U.S. business and real estate.

In other words, in order to raise capital and avoid a recession, we are selling off large chunks of America to foreigners!

Problem Four

The $2.5 Trillion National Debt

The monstrous national debt is also related to the trade deficit. That's because the growth of the national debt is linked directly to interest rates.

The higher interest rates are, the faster the debt grows.

Therefore, if we weren't running such a huge trade deficit, interest rates would be lower . . . and the debt would be less critical.

Problem Five

The Federal Budget Deficits

At the center of the deficit issue is one simple fact: *The federal deficits exist because the U.S. economy cannot grow fast enough to create sufficient tax revenues!*

And the reason the economy can't grow fast enough is that Americans have been buying so many imports.

"In order to raise capital and avoid a recession, we are selling off large chunks of America to foreigners!"

The Reagan administration cut tax rates and created massive federal deficits in an attempt to increase consumer spending and improve the growth of the U.S. economy.

And consumer spending *did* increase; however, a large part of that spending went to buy foreign goods.

As a result, the Reagan tax cut did more to help the economies of Japan and Germany than it did to spur economic growth in the United States.

In effect, the Reagan tax cut helped export American prosperity to our trading partners. . . .

The federal deficits are running far above the Gramm-Rudman target. In fact, 1988's deficits are close to 1986 levels, when the total deficit reached $220 billion! . . .

Problem Six

Recession

The [Bush] administration will face the same problem faced by President Reagan. Expansionary policies that increase spending will lead to even greater imports, a widening trade deficit, higher interest rates, slower economic growth and a continued erosion of the standard of living in America.

That's why the [Reagan] administration has been looking for help abroad. They don't know what else to do—other than badger the Germans and the Japanese to stimulate their economies (and risk inflation) so that we can export more goods to them.

Whether or not we can convince our trading partners to do something, the important thing to recognize is that America is now at the mercy of other nations—more than at any time in our history.

We have to hope that industrialized nations will buy more of what we produce. And we have to hope that Third World nations will pay off their multi-billion dollar loans to our banks.

Otherwise, we may be heading for a severe recessionary downturn.

Problem Seven

Inflation

As the fear of recession grows, so does the probability of runaway inflation.

No one in America—especially a politician—wants to see a long, drawn-out decline of living standards.

To prevent that from happening, Washington has only one alternative: to pour vast quantities of unbacked money into the system.

The Federal Reserve System has already dumped massive sums of money into the economy. And it will have to continue its policy of excessive monetary growth just to keep the slight economic recovery from collapsing.

Unfortunately, adding money to the system will not necessarily improve the health of the U.S. economy. We have already seen how expansionary economic policies can do more good for our international trading partners than for us. As a result, expanding the money supply in an attempt to promote consumer and business spending will do little more than raise the rate of inflation.

The foundation and structure of the world economy has changed. And the changes are dramatic. The most frightening change of all may be the current revolution in economic thinking.

It seems that while everyone was concentrating on the problems of the past few years, "big-government" economics was being reborn.

"Big-government" economics is the belief that the government must *constantly* regulate the economy. In other words, it assumes that if the economy is left on its own, it will self-destruct. It will fall into recession, depression, or inflation.

This "big-government" approach dominated economic thinking from the 1930s to the 1970s. But the massive government spending it justified led to the double-digit inflation of the 1970s.

Then, in the early 1980s, two free-market schools of economic thought—monetarism and supply-side economics—came into the limelight.

"The Reagan tax cut did more to help the economies of Japan and Germany than it did to spur economic growth in the United States."

Monetarist economists argued that massive government spending financed with new money creation would inevitably lead to inflation. Supply-side economists believed that tax cuts would ignite production and boost economic growth.

Both argued for less government interference in the economy. And both were successful—for a while. But the economic stimulation caused by these policies was responsible for exporting American prosperity. And their failures to predict economic events led to the downfall of this free-market economic thinking.

Now that monetarists and the supply siders are gone, "big-government" economics is once again the dominant force in Washington. . . .

A Bleak Future

According to the Stanford economics professor who is an advisor to George Bush: "Free-market theories just haven't succeeded in building a (viable) set of models."

Read that quote carefully. It is a forecast for a bleak future. What it says is that Washington is finished with the idea of a free market. Washington is returning to the days of assuming that the bigger the government is, the better off we will all be.

And that is *exactly* what led to the crisis of the 1970s.

Even more important though, "big-government" economics does not deal with the fact that the international economy now has an impact on virtually every aspect of our domestic economy.

As a result, we're once again on a course that ignores reality and looks to the federal government for a cure to every economic ill.

The growth of the world economy is leading us toward escalating economic disruption, climbing inflation rates, and even greater turmoil in the financial markets.

History has shown that in such an environment, tangible assets are the best investments.

There is, however, one great difference between today and the past. In the past, economic disruption could sometimes be counteracted with domestic policies.

Today, America has almost no control over its own economic destiny. The U.S. is now just one part of the world economy, and our future is no longer in our hands alone.

America's prosperity is already at the mercy of other nations. And unless we allow foreigners to buy up more and more of America, they are likely to pull out their money and run—leaving the U.S. to sink into an economic hole.

We need a turnaround. But there's no telling how or when that will happen. For now, the government has no choice but to rely on money creation and inflation to keep us afloat.

As a result, there is a lot more inflation ahead.

Whether you like it or not, we are already depending on the rest of the world. To survive and prosper you will have to adjust your thinking and your portfolio to that fact.

That's why we believe it is now crucial to build an international portfolio—a portfolio that can benefit from economic growth in other countries and that could, if necessary, be sold anywhere in the world. That means a portfolio with a heavy concentration on tangible assets—precious metals and gold and silver coins—assets that have historically been the basis of wealth preservation in many nations.

We have only to look at 1987 to see what is taking place, because 1987 was the year that the markets finally reacted to the new economic world.

The Bottom Line

Stock markets around the globe are just muddling through. The bull market that pushed U.S. stock prices far above levels justified by either price/earnings ratios or true book value crashed and burned on "Black Monday." And if you look at book value, the DJIA [Dow Jones Industrial Average] could still lose another 50% before it hits bottom.

"Your financial future will be in the hands of faceless foreign investors and politicians."

Meanwhile, investors and governments from every corner of the world are turning to tangible assets. These investors are purchasing gold not only as a hedge against inflation; they are purchasing a traditional asset that they can now afford to buy. That's why gold prices are higher than many predicted.

U.S. economic growth is now dependent on the decisions of foreign politicians and investors.

Your wealth is at the mercy of investment decisions made abroad.

What's more, no one in Washington knows what to do about this crisis! In fact, many are not even willing to admit that it exists. But it does! And it is the single most serious economic threat that you or your children are ever likely to face.

Unless you act immediately to protect yourself, your financial future will be in the hands of faceless foreign investors and politicians.

The Financial Forecaster *is a monthly newsletter published by the Minneapolis investment firm, First Financial Holding Group, Inc.*

"The U.S. was not quite the industrial basket case many made it out to be."

US Industry Is Healthy

Sylvia Nasar

So suddenly that it almost defies belief, the U.S. has seized the lead in the race for global competitiveness. Many of its industries have become the world's low-cost producers. Manufacturers on U.S. soil are gearing up to send Fords to Frankfurt, TVs to Tokyo—perhaps even steel to Seoul. As a result, the export boom now gathering momentum could rival the one that started in 1977 after the dollar fell 25%.

Despite another record trade gap in October 1987, U.S. exports are up 13% and are rising three times faster than world demand. Half the increase in industrial production came from exports—and that was before the dollar's October plunge. As Donald Straszheim of Merrill Lynch puts it: "The U.S., not Japan, is the export-led economy now."

How to account for the sudden reversal? The cheaper dollar, of course. But the currency shift could not do its job had it not been preceded by the gut-wrenching overhaul of industry upon industry, including all-out efforts to raise efficiency, slash costs, make better products, and sell them more aggressively. Finally, it's beginning to become apparent that the U.S. was not quite the industrial basket case many made it out to be.

A caveat: Gains—at home and abroad—will not come as easily this time as they did in the late Seventies, when the U.S. enjoyed a string of trade surpluses that lasted through 1981 by claiming its piece of an ever-expanding pie. Today many imports have made themselves thoroughly at home in the U.S., and markets for exports are growing only sluggishly. U.S. companies will have to grab market share back from competitors who are much tougher now. Among them are Latin American and East Asian newly industrialized countries (NICs) that can pick up new technologies almost as fast as they are developed in the major industrial nations. But barring highly improbable reversals—a resurgence of the dollar, a relapse on the part of U.S. industry—the U.S. should be able to recapture a great deal of business. The physical volume of the trade deficit turned long ago, and the dollar balance will follow as rising import prices start hitting sales harder.

There's no question that the dollar's decline is the chief player in the new competitiveness drama. Today it is back to where it was in the days when the U.S. ran healthy trade surpluses. On the trade-weighted index of the dollar vs. ten currencies compiled by the Federal Reserve, the dollar now stands just about at its 1980 value. Since U.S. exporters haven't raised their dollar prices much, overseas customers have been handed a discount that amounts to rolling back prices five or six years.

A 1980 Dollar

True, the dollar has weakened only a little or not at all against the currencies of partners that account for roughly half of U.S. trade: Latin America, Canada, and the newly industrialized countries of the Pacific Rim (except for the Taiwan dollar, which has appreciated about 37% since 1985). What that observation overlooks is that the dollar did not strengthen much against these currencies in the first place. The modest weakening has put the dollar back where it was in 1980.

The new currency relationships powerfully boost the ability of the U.S. to compete with virtually all its major trading partners. It now has a clear edge over European manufacturers. They account for about a quarter of U.S. trade, with the U.S. importing shoes, cars, aircraft, organic chemicals, and machinery and exporting aircraft, computers, and chemicals. In West Germany current trends are working heavily against exporters. Though many are moving to restructure, particularly in the metals and

Sylvia Nasar, "America's Competitive Revival," *Fortune*, January 4, 1988.
© 1988 Time Inc. All rights reserved.

capital goods industries, wages are advancing at a rate of 4.5% to 5% a year and productivity is stagnating.

Japan's tremendous price advantage has all but disappeared: Manufacturing costs are about the same now as in the U.S. The Japanese are responding with breathtaking speed by holding down wage increases and boosting productivity. The strong yen, moreover, is slashing the cost of imported raw materials such as coal and iron ore. But these trends cannot wipe out the effects of the huge appreciation. The U.S., whose exports to Japan have been concentrated in aircraft, computers, organic chemicals, and pharmaceuticals, will now be able to export more cars, steel, and machine tools.

The U.S. is at least as competitive against Canada, its largest trading partner, as it was at the start of the Eighties. The Canadian dollar is about 12% weaker than in 1980, but unit labor costs have risen more than in the U.S. The trade deficit with Canada has increased chiefly because of faster U.S. growth, especially the five-year surge in auto sales. American carmakers build components, large cars, and minivans in Ontario to take advantage of cheaper labor and energy costs.

American competitiveness has improved least against the NICs, which account for nearly as much of U.S. manufactured goods trade as the Europeans. Labor costs are a fraction of those in industrialized countries. Productivity is rising rapidly. And so are these countries' manufacturing savvy and production capacity. Even so, U.S. exports to the NICs should grow since they include many components for assembly and re-export, some destined for third countries.

"The U.S. is still the world's biggest producer in most major industries."

No one should be surprised or dismayed that the competition is tougher today than it used to be. "That's what we mean by economic development in the rest of the world," says William Branson, an economist at the International Monetary Fund. Since the late Fifties, other countries have been closing the gigantic lead in economic power held by the U.S. at the end of World War II. Productivity, real wages, and profitability in manufacturing have been growing faster abroad than in the U.S. Similarly, the American edge in technology—in everything from spacecraft to supercomputers—has shrunk. Americans can no longer claim to make the best of everything: Others now build better cars, 256K D-Rams, TVs, and high-performance machine tools, to name just a few.

But the major causes of today's trade deficit lie in forces that manufacturers could not control—the strong dollar, powerful U.S. domestic demand, and the collapse of Latin American export markets due to those countries' heavy debts.

The Biggest Producer

It is easy to forget that the U.S. is still the world's biggest producer in most major industries, among them aluminum, paper, aircraft, and computers. It is the technology leader in computers, scientific instruments, and telecommunications equipment. Its overall factory productivity is still the highest, though Japan has passed it in such industries as autos and electronics. And its industrial production has risen faster in the Eighties than in most other countries.

Lately, capital investment has been more robust than is generally appreciated. Capacity has expanded by one-fourth since 1979, more rapidly than in other industrialized countries. Walter Cadette, an economist at Morgan Guaranty, points out that the ratio of net capital stock to labor has recently been rising at its historical trend rate of 3% a year in manufacturing. Says Cadette: "That's strong evidence that the comeback of productivity isn't a one-shot deal."

What's more, the aggregate investment figures hide an important change: Resources have shifted out of declining industries and into growing ones. For example, since 1979 capacity fell by 25% in steel, was flat in nonferrous metals, and increased a mere 5% in textiles. Meantime capacity soared 35% in instruments, 40% in computers and other so-called nonelectrical machinery, and 59% in electric machinery and components.

All this said, the U.S. did lose its fighting edge during the late Seventies. Productivity growth collapsed and costs raged out of control, rising some 40% between 1977 and 1981—far faster than abroad. All the while, those foreign competitors were getting tougher.

The critical changes began when the economy went into the tank and the dollar took off during the early Eighties. Company after company was forced to close inefficient plants and modernize others, spin off product lines it couldn't manage well, shed layers of bureaucracy, and trim the work force. What began as a desperate struggle for survival now looks increasingly like a sea change: a new managerial atmosphere in which competition at home and abroad forces continuous efforts to whittle costs, ratchet up quality, and develop new products.

Often the changes were spurred by corporate raiders and takeover threats. Unlike merger waves of the past, where the goals were diversifying, integrating vertically, or reducing competition, the restructuring wave of the Eighties was aimed at undoing an accretion of earlier bad strategic decisions—for example, promiscuous conglomeration. In most cases, says Robert Gay, senior economist at

Morgan Stanley, financial restructuring went hand in hand with drives to improve efficiency and cut costs. More than half the mergers and acquisitions activity of this decade, according to a Morgan Stanley study, was concentrated in manufacturing, where international competition is hottest, though manufacturing accounts for just one-fifth of the nation's output.

A Classic Case

The restructuring of the American pulp and paper business is a classic case. It enjoys comparative advantages galore. With a $110 billion domestic market, the industry can achieve tremendous economies of scale. Then there are all those fast-sprouting Southern pines, which mature in half the time it takes northern types. Japan, Scandinavia, and Canada, the largest producers after the U.S., can't expand capacity in commodity paper products because they cannot increase their raw materials supplies enough, says security analyst Mark Rogers at Prudential-Bache.

But nature alone can't grow the fattest profit margins in the world, and plenty of other countries were giving the U.S. a hard time even before the dollar took off. The Finns have offset their high costs by pioneering new technologies. The Brazilians, with abundant, cheap power supplies, are the low-cost pulp producers.

The phenomenal restructuring wave that swept America, swallowing giants like Crown Zellerbach, St. Regis, and Diamond International, has rationalized product lines, held down compensation, and retired old machinery. Analysts figure that a significant part of the industry's earnings explosion since early 1986 can be traced to the greater efficiency and cost consciousness restructuring brought. Today the industry boasts some of the most modern facilities, probably the highest productivity, and quite possibly the fiercest cost-cutting management in the world. These strengths, and the dollar's fall, are helping manufacturers regain overseas markets, especially in Europe and Japan.

A notably bad habit partly combed out of the American system during the upheavals of the Eighties was the self-indulgence of pay increases unmatched by productivity gains. For workers and middle managers, if not top executives, the changes have been dramatic. Manufacturing compensation, which had been rising 10% a year during most of the Seventies and outpaced gains in the rest of the economy, slowed to less than 2.5% a year by the mid-Eighties.

A Slower Rate of Growth

More important, compensation has been growing at a slower rate in the U.S. than abroad, and the trends have produced stunning shifts. German workers now earn about 25% more per hour than

U.S. workers, says Roger Brinner, chief economist at Data Resources. In 1984 they earned 25% less. Japanese workers still get less pay than U.S. workers but the gap is narrowing: Today they earn 85% as much, vs. just 50% in 1984.

The steel industry was a paradigm of the case for wage restraint. For years management gave away the store to keep the labor peace; by 1982 average compensation, at $23 an hour, was 85% above the U.S. manufacturing average and barely on the same planet with rates in other countries. That has all changed. Compensation hasn't risen a nickel since 1982. Moderate wage increases from here on won't turn big steel back into a growth industry—20 million tons of capacity must still be cut in the U.S. alone. But along with work-rule changes, modernization, and the savage restructuring that has cut employment and capacity, they will help to keep the industry in business.

"German workers now earn about 25% more per hour than U.S. workers."

Productivity in U.S. steel trails that of Germany, but is now as high as in Japan. Labor costs per ton—the primary criterion of international competitiveness—were nearly three times costs in Japan or Germany in 1982. Now they have started to converge with those in other industrialized countries, according to John Jacobson, an analyst at the WEFA Group economic consulting firm. The real challenge, says Jacobson, is to displace German and Japanese exports in third markets. Since the U.S. now ranks 20th in exports, behind a cluster of African nations, such a development seems unlikely. Still, hope springs eternal. In a joint venture with Korea's Pohang Steel, USX will overhaul a West Coast plant (in, naturally, Pittsburg, California) to supply sheet to nearby appliance and can plants. Says Earle McIntire, a spokesman for USS/Posco Industries: "We also see some opportunities for exporting from here to the Pacific Rim. It would be a neat thing to pull off." Sure would.

Along with cutting costs, U.S. manufacturers are scoring powerful productivity gains. Since 1981 U.S. manufacturing productivity has been growing faster than that of other industrialized countries. Its long-term trend, around 3.5% a year, is nearly twice the rate of the late Seventies and matches that of the Sixties.

Productivity growth has been fastest in such heavily restructured industries as autos, where output per hour has been rising 6% a year since 1981. Ford, for example, turned out 10% more cars in 1987 than it did in 1978, with 47% fewer production workers. A recent study of 38 car assembly plants in 13 countries by John Krafcik, an auto consultant at MIT [Massachusetts Institute of Technology], showed that U.S. plants no longer lag behind the Japanese in productivity across the board. Incredibly, some American plants—and relatively ordinary ones, at that, with no ranked masses of robots—had higher productivity than many of their counterparts in Japan.

Greater efficiency has helped lower production costs. At current exchange rates, the famous $2,500 cost gap between cars made in Detroit and in Toyota City has disappeared. And costs are 5% to 10% lower than in Europe. That is an added incentive— apart from import quotas—for Japanese and even Korean carmakers to set up American factories. By 1990 Japan will have built ten such plants producing 2.5 million cars, either in partnership with U.S. companies or on their own—the equivalent of another Chrysler. . . .

"The companies that met the trials of the early Eighties most successfully . . . have emerged as industry leaders."

The U.S. would pay a high price for losing the momentum it has gained. The unsustainable trade deficit would demand a much steeper fall in the dollar, swelling inflation and further diminishing competitiveness. Then hard times would arrive with a vengeance. The U.S. could stay competitive only if its wages fell, shrinking American living standards and, perhaps, forcing the nation to export the fruits of low-wage labor—the NIC syndrome—to settle its trade accounts.

But in general the companies that met the trials of the early Eighties most successfully did so by fundamentally changing their management philosophies, and they have emerged as industry leaders. At the same time the U.S. market, which was still insular back in the Seventies, has become the world's most competitive. As more foreign companies set up their new factories on American soil, the competition will grow hotter yet. In such an environment, those reborn managers seem most unlikely to fall from grace again.

Sylvia Nasar is an associate editor of Fortune *magazine.*

"The manufacturing sector of the U.S. economy is in decline."

US Industry Is Declining

John Miller and Ramon Castellblanch

Blue-collar workers, unlike economic policy makers, have never had a hard time believing the United States is deindustrializing. More than five million manufacturing workers lost their jobs permanently between 1981 and 1985 thanks to plant closings and layoffs. Meanwhile, the new jobs created during the 1980s have been lower paying, service-sector jobs.

Until recently, many policy makers continued to call deindustrialization a myth. While most analysts now agree that the manufacturing sector of the U.S. economy is in decline, many still maintain that the trend is a natural step in the maturation of a capitalist economy and represents no impediment to future growth.

Liberal policy analysts see manufacturing's decline more as a sign the U.S. economy has entered its dotage than as a sign of maturation. They argue that a healthy manufacturing sector does indeed matter for the long-term health of the U.S. economy and that the vision of a prosperous post-industrial service economy is fantasy.

Does manufacturing matter? Will a policy dedicated to reviving U.S. manufacturing produce a period of sustained economic growth in the United States and recapture the high-wage jobs lost in basic manufacturing? Will a policy that fosters a post-industrial economy do any better? More importantly, would either policy offer relief for those who have suffered directly from the disruptions of deindustrialization?

While there may still be controversy about the permanence and significance of the decline of manufacturing, the trend is real and measurable. The United States is, in fact, deindustrializing.

Since the mid-1970s, deindustrialization has been part of the national consciousness. Steel towns became ghost towns as the international economy became increasingly competitive and U.S. corporations went out of business or moved their operations abroad. The 1982 recession, which ravaged the industrial heartland, made a bad thing worse. Employment in manufacturing declined from 27.3% of the non-agricultural work force in 1973, at the peak of the postwar boom, to 19.5% in 1985. Even in absolute terms, there were fewer manufacturing workers in 1985 than in 1973. The traditional manufacturing industries that had been the engine for postwar prosperity—autos, textiles, steel, and apparel—were particularly hard hit, losing 12% of their workers between 1980 and 1986.

Many conservative policy makers denied the deindustrialization trend. Citing Commerce Department data now recognized as inaccurate, they argued that manufacturing's share of real output in the 1980s remained essentially unchanged at about 22% of GNP [gross national product], close to its postwar average. Corrected figures from the Congressional Office of Technology Assessment, however, showed that manufacturing's share of output has declined significantly: from 22% in 1977 to 18% in 1987.

Conservative Rationalizations

Once deindustrialization could no longer be denied, conservative policy analysts offered two rationalizations. First, they argued that the decline in manufacturing and the broader economy did not represent a permanent shift but was temporary, directly attributable to the overvalued dollar of the early 1980s.

There is some truth to this argument. In the 1970s, U.S. manufacturing ran substantial trade surpluses in capital goods, chemicals, and military goods, while experiencing deficits in consumer goods such as motor vehicles and textiles. By the 1980s, as the

John Miller and Ramon Castellblanch, "Does Manufacturing Matter?" *Dollars & Sense*, October 1988. Reprinted with permission.

value of the dollar increased and the economies of U.S. trading partners grew more slowly, the U.S. trade balance turned negative in almost every manufacturing category.

Today's lower value of the dollar is slowly reviving some of those manufacturing industries that were competitive in the 1970s, but deindustrialization persists in those industries that lost their competitive edge prior to 1980. The lower dollar alone can do little to make industries such as consumer goods, autos, or steel competitive again in the near future.

The other conservative rationalization for the loss of manufacturing was best presented by President Reagan in a 1985 report to Congress. "The move from an industrial society toward a post-industrial service economy has been one of the greatest changes to affect the developed world since the Industrial Revolution," Reagan told legislators. "The progression of an economy such as America's from agricultural to manufacturing to services is a natural change."

The argument is simple: as incomes rise, consumer demand naturally shifts away from manufacturing toward services. And as productivity increases in manufacturing, the demand for manufacturing workers automatically decreases.

The argument is also unsupported. First, real family incomes are not rising, lifting us into post-industrial bliss; they are now lower than they were in the early 1970s. Second, the U.S. economy is not just losing manufacturing *jobs*; manufacturing's share of total output has also declined, indicating that more is at work than just productivity increases.

"The U.S. economy is not just losing manufacturing jobs; manufacturing's share of total output has also declined."

Nonetheless, the implicit premise of those who advocate a post-industrial economy is persuasive. They hold that the contribution to economic growth of a dollar's worth of output is the same, regardless of the sector that produces it, be it manufacturing or services. For them, manufacturing matters no more than any other sector, and, in fact, is not required (or perhaps even desirable) for future economic development.

History would disagree. While they overstate the argument, advocates of reindustrialization argue correctly that in the past, manufacturing industries possessed properties for generating broad-based economic growth that many services industries did not possess.

Historically, manufacturing has been the engine of capitalist development. An increasing share of manufacturing output has gone hand-in-hand with

sustained economic growth and rapid gains in productivity. This association has held from the industrial revolution in England to the postwar U.S. economy, and it is still evident in the development patterns of third world countries today.

One of the keys to this association are the productivity gains from the innovation that predominates in manufacturing. Productivity levels, as traditionally measured by the value-added per hour worked, have, in fact, been higher in manufacturing than in the rest of the economy, especially in the last decade.

Value-Added Factor

The value-added in an industry is the difference between the cost of inputs other than labor and the sales revenues the industry collects. The difference represents the income an industry generates. Only when the value-added is relatively high is there significant income to distribute between corporate profits on the one hand, and wages and salaries on the other. For example, until the mid-1970s, the high value-added in the steel industry, along with the dominance of U.S. companies in the world market and the militant unionism of steel workers, produced the high-wage jobs that predominated in the industry. There was a relatively large pie over which labor and management could fight.

In 1986, productivity in manufacturing (as measured by value-added) was $20.27 per hour compared to $18.08 for all private services averaged together. Within the service sector, the value-added measures were highest for those services closely related to manufacturing—business and professional services, transportation, wholesale trade, and warehousing. For services not closely tied to manufacturing—consumer services, social services, and retail trade—the value-added was much lower: in the range of $12 to $13 per hour.

Higher-than-average value-added in certain manufacturing industries has allowed higher wages for some workers. Manufacturing wages as a whole, in fact, have been higher than those in the rest of the economy throughout the postwar period. For instance, in 1984, total compensation for manufacturing workers averaged $28,700 while total compensation for service workers was considerably less: $22,900. While workers in services more closely linked to manufacturing did better—about $24,600—they still made less than manufacturing workers.

Beyond considerations of productivity, critics of the post-industrial economy point to the dependence of a broad range of services on manufacturing, making a prosperous post-industrial service economy an economic and technological impossibility. Services, they argue, are complements to manufacturing, not substitutes or successors. "What we're saying is that if you lose manufacturing you will lose the high-wage service jobs," argue Stephen

Cohen and John Zysman, authors of the book, *Manufacturing Matters*. According to Cohen and Zysman, some 25% of this country's GNP is produced by services that are "tightly linked" to manufacturing—insurance, accounting, transportation, etc.

In addition, productivity increases in services in the past have come about from the introduction of manufactured products into the provision of services. The productivity of the modern office, for example, was greatly enhanced by the computer, a manufactured good.

Historic Contribution

A further economic consideration in the post-industrial scenario is the historic contribution of manufacturing to the country's balance of payments. When manufacturing was healthy, the United States ran a substantial trade surplus. Since the early 1980s, the trade deficit has become a serious dilemma. Of 1987's $171 billion trade deficit, $138 billion was in manufacturing. The United States ran a small surplus in services, but this is small consolation. Because services have to be supplied locally, they are less easily traded internationally. It is extremely unlikely the United States can make up for the importation of manufactured goods with the exportation of services.

Cohen and Zysman are perhaps the most influential of a significant group of policy makers and activists calling for a federal program to revitalize the manufacturing sector. While they are right that the vibrant post-industrial economy is wishful thinking, many of their points are overstated. The problem—and the challenge—goes beyond the confines of the manufacturing sector. There is no doubt that high-wage jobs have been concentrated in manufacturing and that deindustrialization has led to a proliferation of low-wage jobs. But there is more at work here than the alleged magic of manufacturing.

In fact, high productivity is only one of several factors contributing to high wages in an industry. The high wages that predominated in the steel and auto industries, for example, resulted not just from high productivity but from the relative dominance of U.S. companies in the world market. Freed from the intense pressure of competition, U.S. corporations could set prices at levels high enough to guarantee high profits and allow wage increases.

Nor should we forget the role labor itself played in fighting for those increases. The tradition of militant unionism within the auto and steel industries had a great deal to do with the wage levels attained by the mid-1970s. And such gains are not limited to manufacturing. Unionized hotel workers have raised their pay significantly through collective action. Current efforts to combat gender discrimination in wage levels can also raise salaries, particularly in service-sector jobs.

While productivity is a factor in allowing wage gains, the value-added measure itself tends to overstate real productivity. Because it is impossible to compare dissimilar products, value-added is based on the dollar value of output, not the physical output. As a result, products with inflated prices or underpriced inputs automatically report higher value-added even though their physical productivity may be no higher. In addition, valued-added is often measured only indirectly, by adding wages and profits in an industry. Higher-than-average wages then translate into higher-than-average productivity, when in fact what is being measured may be monopoly price-setting and militant unionism.

If services were as unionized as manufacturing and service work was recognized as having comparable value to manufacturing work, and if service industries had as much monopoly control over prices as some manufacturing industries have had, then value-added and wages in services would come much closer to the levels in manufacturing.

Services vs. Manufacturing

The debate over the significance of manufacturing for future economic growth is important because it refocuses attention on the role the government plays in promoting, guiding, or, alternately, discouraging investment. No matter how loudly government officials proclaim the "freedom" of the marketplace, the government is constantly intervening in the economy. Such intervention is never neutral and should be open to public scrutiny.

"The debate over the significance of manufacturing for future economic growth is important."

But it would be a mistake to limit industrial policy to the manufacturing sector, just as it would be a mistake to treat the manufacturing sector as one homogeneous group equally deserving of government support. Some service industries, such as public utilities, have higher value-added than many manufacturing industries. Conversely, some low-wage manufacturing industries, such as costume jewelry, have lower value-added than most services. Also, given increased international competition, some manufacturing industries that have declined in recent years are unlikely to revive. We should not be trying to save sunset manufacturing industries at any cost: the cost may well be too high and the potential for reviving the industry too low.

To formulate a progressive industrial policy, we must look beyond the broad categories of manufacturing and services to specific industries. Among the factors to consider are the potential productivity of an industry; its potential competitive position in the world market; its potential degree of unionization; its linkages to other industries; and its social utility. (The last point is important: many military manufacturers have high value-added, while child-care centers do not, but we would hardly support the former over the latter.)

Progressives should keep in mind that the goal of industrial policy is not to revive the postwar boom; in today's world economy, that is impossible. The goal is to bring about a different type of growth directed not by profits and private investment, but by wages and economic planning.

Since World War II, the United States has not had an explicit industrial policy to guide public investment in the economy. Instead, postwar industrial policy has been implicit but active, favoring military manufacturers and, more recently, financial services. With the continued erosion of high-wage jobs and the proliferation of low-wage employment, now is the time to advocate an industrial policy that promotes the standard of living of all working people.

John Miller teaches economics at Wheaton College in Illinois. Ramon Castellblanch is a health-care consultant for labor unions in California.

"Our economic crisis 'cannot be resolved without releasing resources now claimed by our bloated military budget.'"

Theodore Lownik Library
Illinois Benedictine College
Lisle, Illinois 60532

Defense Spending Has Harmed the Economy

The Washington Spectator

Washington now realizes, reluctantly, the time has come to pay the piper. The bill, a debt of nearly $2½ trillion with a yearly interest payment of more than $150 billion, rose in part on extravagances—useless wars, terrifying weapons of mass destruction and a tax cut.

"In preparing for the war that must never come, the U.S. has spent more than two trillion dollars in the last six years alone." (*Beyond War*) The tax cut took a big bite out of government revenues. The loss in one year alone, fiscal 1987, was $238.5 billion.

The effect: The national debt has doubled. Because of the emphasis on guns rather than civilian goods, "the U.S. is forced to acknowledge that its period of unchallenged leadership [as an industrial power] is over." (*Financial Times*) Some two million well-paying factory jobs have been lost during this period.

The alternative to paying the piper is an economic nightmare: inflation, mass bankruptcies, more job losses, and a government without the wherewithal to operate.

While there is agreement in Washington on the need to cut back, there are multiple differences about how to do this. President Reagan, ever the idle dreamer, would wish the deficit away. Some in Congress would raise taxes; others would prune the budget.

Actually, the simplest and most direct strategy is to take a meat ax to military spending, according to a detailed three-year study by World Policy Institute. It insists that "one trillion dollars can be safely shifted over the next 10 years from U.S. military budgets." In the first five years, $374.4 billion could be saved, a sum much larger than figures mentioned on Capitol Hill today. The Institute states that our economic crisis "cannot be resolved without releasing resources now claimed by our bloated military budget."

The goal can be reached by giving up our role as world cop. The authoritative Center for Defense Information estimates that only 7 to 8% of our $320 billion annual military cost is for the defense of North America.

Enough Guns for Defense

The Institute's proposal would provide enough guns and men to defend the U.S. and to maintain a watch on aggressive movements across the world. For example, it would reduce the Administration goal of strategic nuclear weapons by 1992 of 2,126 to 842; drop tactical nuclear weapons from 18,000 to 10,000, warheads from 14,394 to 8,394, ground forces from 12 divisions to 8, naval forces from 400 ships to 350, Air Force wings from 45 to 25.

This program, in effect, would throw out the "manifest destiny" policy that dictates U.S. foreign policy. The term was used in 1845 by John L. O'Sullivan in the *New York Morning News*: It is our "manifest destiny to go forth as a world conqueror. . . . This is what fate holds for the chosen people." This has tickled the vanity of Americans over the years and led us to a series of not always distinguished military operations abroad. Mark Twain was inspired to outrage by our Philippines campaign.

After WWII, the U.S. took on a broad mission, to bring prosperity and freedom to the world and repel the demons of communism. The inevitable result was war. To satisfy the "manifest destiny," we plunged into war in Korea and Vietnam, with military excursions in Central America, Libya and the Persian Gulf. At the same time, we engaged in a titanic buildup of weapons. The bill has been enormous in lives, money and scarce resources. American casualties in Vietnam were 211,324. The cost of Reagan's "Star Wars" is estimated at $1

The Washington Spectator, "Time To Pay the Piper," January 1, 1988. Reprinted with permission.

trillion. Recently the General Accounting Office found that the B1 bomber program will cost $6 billion more than the Administration's estimate, for a total of $28.3 billion. A new expense, the Persian Gulf operation, cost $69 million from mid-July through September 30, 1987.

Resources, workers and scientific talent needed to modernize our industry went into the war machine. West Germany and Japan, with no "manifest destiny," put in new machinery—thanks to us—and took away world markets.

The U.S. spends 6.7% of its gross national product on the military, while West Germany spends but 3.1%, reports the chairman of the House Intelligence Committee, Rep. Lee H. Hamilton (D-Ind.). Economic demographer Bernard Windham declares that the national debt piled up by Reagan, more than under all previous Presidents combined, "is primarily due to the unprecedented military buildup—more than doubling of defense expenditures."

A New Diet

It will not be easy for the political community to give up "manifest destiny" and take on a humbler diet. President Reagan is a born-again believer in "manifest destiny." On Capitol Hill, there is a myth that the electorate is sold on big military spending. However, a national poll taken in October 1987 shows that "economic strength has replaced military strength as the primary criterion for defining national strength." (World Policy Institute) Only 18% of those polled linked U.S. strength to the military; 85% favored cuts in military budgets by asking Japan, Korea and West Europe to pay for their own defense.

The *Washington Post*'s political writer, David S. Broder, found a general "disquiet . . . a fear that there would be a day of reckoning" for the economy. Today, polls show that the "disquiet" focuses on military spending and operations. Rep. Anthony C. Beilenson (D-Ca.) questioned his constituents and discovered that 70% disagreed "with the President's decision to go ahead with his plan for early deployment of the Strategic Defense Initiative [SDI]." Also, 71% opposed further aid for the Nicaraguan contras and 69% were against the Persian Gulf operation. . . .

One reason for the peculiar blindness of the Washington politician is the military-industrial complex and its pervasive lobbying.

The power of the lobby is shown by the *Cleveland Plain Dealer*: "Defense contractors' prices are raised to unrealistic levels and are included as the 'costs of doing business.' The Government pays for all the costs the company incurs selling the weapons, the company's research and development and manufacturing, and then guarantees the company a profit. Even when companies use Government

buildings, funds and equipment, the design plans become property of the defense contractor. . . . Defense contractors accused of criminal fraud but not convicted have been permitted to bill the Federal Government for millions of dollars in legal fees and also have been allowed to add an additional fee for corporate profits. . . . Many of the weapons systems produced don't work, yet they are rarely cancelled; payment for these systems is made two days to one week after the bill is submitted. . . . Fully one-half to nearly all of the salaries of the defense contractors' top executives—$500,000 to one million dollars annual income—is paid by the taxpayer. In addition, special savings accounts and generous pension programs are paid by the Government. Bonuses to top executives are included in the cost of the programs and help to drive up the costs of future defense projects. . . . The Defense Contracts Audit Agency can only point out improper charges, not stop them. While the Pentagon provides contractors with unlimited funds, the Justice Department conducts 'scanty' investigations due to limited funds."

The "Star Wars" Fantasy

President Reagan's pet military project, "Star Wars," is a case in point. It is the product of a powerful lobby and a lively imagination. Some quotes:

"'Star Wars' is a classic example of dangerous self-delusion proceeding from a dreamy lack of contact with reality." (Former Air Force Undersecretary Townsend Hoopes)

"The Reagan Administration has ignored the best scientific advice, spurned Soviet arms control initiatives, and rushed ahead with a dangerous and expensive gamble." (Union of Concerned Scientists)

"A perfect defense is not a realistic thing." (Lt. Gen. James Abrahamson)

"One reason for the peculiar blindness of the Washington politician is the military-industrial complex and its pervasive lobbying."

"This is probably the biggest project this country has ever been asked to fund. You don't even have an idea [how much it will cost]. . . . We are faced, in my opinion, with a threat far more destructive than anything Russia might throw at us in missiles, and that is our deficit." (Former Senator Barry Goldwater, R-Ariz.)

"There are many of us in the military, both active and retired, who believe that the effect of a 'Star Wars' system would be to destroy our national security by greatly increasing the likelihood of nuclear war." (Dr. Robert Bowman, former head of the Advanced Space Program Development for the Pentagon)

"One of the first casualties of SDI, if we are not careful . . . is likely to be arms control." (Brent Scowcroft, [present] National Security Advisor and [former] arms negotiator)

"Near term SDI deployment is an absurd and dangerous course for America. It would force us to break the bank, throw out the ABM [antiballistic missile] treaty, and commit us to an arms race in space. And for what? . . . This is not a military shield, it is a political ploy." (Senator J. Bennett Johnson, D-La., member of Senate Defense Appropriations Subcommittee)

The Trade Deficit

The way "manifest destiny" and big military spending has crippled our economy is shown in a comparison with Japan. The U.S. is spending 7.14% of its gross national product on combined defense and foreign aid; Japan, 1.29%. "The U.S. has not only assumed the military protection of the Japanese islands, but has also assumed a major burden in protecting Japanese interests throughout the world," says Senator John McCain (R-Ariz.). He points out that "the Japanese oil supply lines are being protected by the U.S. Navy, Air Force and Marine Corps at a cost of $1 million a day" in the Persian Gulf. Japan gets 60% of its oil supply from there; we get 7%.

Japan has an $81 billion trade surplus; we have a $185 billion trade deficit.

Why? An article in the Buenos Aires newsmagazine *Siete Dias* offers an explanation. The city of Tsukuba, 42 miles northeast of Tokyo, has an "almost holy significance." Here, kamikazes trained for suicide missions against the U.S. invasion fleet. Today, the city has been transformed into "a factory for ideas . . . the most important scientific research center in history." Not for military gizmos, but to "take the lead in fields such as microelectronics, robotics, optics and chemicals," areas in which the U.S. had once been dominant.

An ironic side note here: "Four decades after the Bank of America became the first U.S. bank to provide financing to rebuild Japan's war-torn economy, nine Japanese banks agreed to come to the stricken giant's aid by investing $130 million in its corporate parent, BankAmerica." (*Los Angeles Times*)

Japan has an $81 billion trade surplus; we have a $185 billion trade deficit. Why? Japan's emphasis is on non-military research.

At the same time, much of U.S. science and many universities are engaged in non-productive military research. So, "we saw a trade deficit escalating from $42 billion in 1981 to a stunning $170 billion in 1986. The Reagan recovery seemed to be based on buying imported goods and borrowing the money

from abroad to pay for them. . . . It is an inescapable fact that a nation cannot buy $3 billion more from abroad every week than it sells—and hope to remain a prosperous nation over the long term." (Senator John D. Rockefeller IV, D-W.Va.)

The *AFL-CIO News* adds another sobering fact: "economists estimate that America loses some 22,500 jobs for every $1 million in imports that enter the domestic market. Since President Reagan came to office, more than two million factory jobs have been washed away by the rising import tide."

In an *Atlantic Monthly* article, Peter G. Peterson tells what has happened to the two million who lost their jobs: "More than a third of them remain indefinitely out of work; more than half the rest have taken pay cuts of 30 to 50% in new jobs that cannot make use of their experience." It is no wonder that the August 1987 trade deficit, $15.7 billion ($17.6 billion in October), set off the October market plunge and sent the dollar lower.

"Japan has an $81 billion trade surplus; we have a $185 billion trade deficit. Why? Japan's emphasis is on non-military research."

Tsukuba, the Japanese science city, is devoted to developing a lead in non-military areas. For example: "In the Tsukuba electronic laboratory, one of 46 institutes in the science city that also encompasses two universities, Hisao Hayakawas plays with a tiny square that sticks to the end of his fingers. It is an integrated switch 10 to 100 times faster than any of the conventional computers." (Buenos Aires newsmagazine *Siete Dias*)

Hunger in America

A study by the Physicians Task Force on Hunger in America finds that 20 million Americans, particularly workers dropped from manufacturing jobs and now in service areas, as well as infants and the elderly, do not get enough to eat.

The report looked at places that were until recent years scenes of blue-collar prosperity—Texas oil fields, factory and mining towns. In Texas, for example, requests for food relief have doubled since 1983, to 3.6 million. At the same time, real wages have dropped. Average weekly earnings at the end of June 1987 were $169, measured in 1977 dollars. In 1962, they were $172, measured in the same way.

The spread of unemployment has affected business. The *San Francisco Chronicle* reports, for example, that "northern Californians are outpacing the nation in an unprecedented rush to insolvency, with a 41% increase in personal bankruptcy filings in 1986." Washington's insensitivity to this plight is suggested by a *New York Times* story that appeared October 16, 1987: "The Reagan Administration has adopted a new policy that will reduce welfare payments for many elderly, blind and disabled people who receive free food, shelter, firewood and winter clothing from churches and charitable organizations." The non-cash assistance must be counted as income under the Supplemental Security Income program.

What Are the Answers?

One tried and true tactic for revising a sick economy is to lower interest rates. This ordinarily brings a boom in large-ticket items, such as homes, cars, refrigerators, TV sets. But this is no longer valid, because the U.S. relies on foreign investors to keep the Treasury solvent. MIT [Massachusetts Institute of Technology] economist Lester Thurow points out, "In 1980, we had a trade account surplus of $166 billion; by August 1987, we had an indebtedness to foreigners of $340 billion." (*New Perspectives Quarterly*) If foreign investors pull out, "the U.S., in response, would have little choice but to raise interest rates sky-high, in order to attract at least some investors to finance our budget deficits." (*Atlantic Monthly*)

"We are moving into an era 'when economic strength, not military power, increasingly determines a nation's influence in the world.'"

The only way out is to button up, pay the piper and take the advice of the World Policy Institute. It would cut the military, "based on a more realistic assessment of the security threats we face, the greatly diminished utility of the projection of military power to advance the country's interests, and the increased ability of our allies to organize their own defense." We are moving into an era "when economic strength, not military power, increasingly determines a nation's influence in the world. . . . The new thinking in Moscow, with its emphasis on economic modernization and on expanding political and economic relations, provides the U.S. an opportunity."

In other words, toss out "manifest destiny," reach an agreement with the Soviets to cut back on costly weapons—which Moscow dearly needs, also—take care of the victims of the economic storm, and learn to live on a pay-as-you-go basis.

The Washington Spectator *is a semimonthly publication of The Public Concern Foundation, a public policy research organization in Fairfax, Virginia.*

"That the U.S. economy is or soon will be in decline...from the country's excessive military burdens...is a quite incredible idea."

viewpoint 17

Defense Spending Has Little Effect on the Economy

Herbert Stein

Almost every day one reads in the newspaper an op-ed page article predicting, or warning of, the decline of America. Usually the decline is said to have its source in the relative economic weakening of this country. And that, in turn, is now fashionably ascribed to our "heavy military burdens." The lesson drawn is that the United States should reduce its military burdens or, less prescriptively, will have to do so. The United States will have to move over and surrender or share world leadership ("hegemony" is the word of art).

The source or support for much of this talk is a book by Professor Paul Kennedy of Yale, *The Rise and Fall of the Great Powers* (Random House, 1987). The theme of this book as summarized by Hodding Carter in a *Wall Street Journal* article is: "The history of great powers is marked first by economic dynamism that takes them to the top, then decline caused by mounting military burdens that erode and then destroy the economic base that first created the power."

Thus we have the hypothesis of a Kennedy curve, which is a historical counterpart of the Laffer curve. Kennedy describes the rise of powers as propelled by rising economic strength and the fall of powers as caused by military burdens that topple what had been the rising economic curve. Similarly the Laffer curve depicted government revenues as being higher the higher tax rates are until tax rates reached a certain critical point above which higher tax rates yielded lower and lower revenue. Once the hypothesis is accepted, in either the Kennedy or the Laffer case, the critical question is where we actually are. Are we on the rising or falling part of the curve? Many politicians and other amateurs assumed, as soon as the Laffer curve was brought to

their attention, that the United States was on the falling part of the curve. But that was wrong. Similarly, the assumption of many commentators is that the United States is on the declining part of the Kennedy curve. But that, of course, is something to be investigated, not assumed. In my opinion this assumption flies in the face of the facts.

Relative Economic Capability

The notion of power, of being at the top, indicates that we are interested in *relative* economic capability—in the economic capability of the United States compared with that of other countries. The comparison with adversaries is particularly relevant. . . .

What stands out, aside from the estimate that the GDP [gross domestic product] of the USSR is less than 60 percent of the GDP of the United States, is the relative size of China's. But the main import is the inadequacy of GDP as a measure of economic strength. China's ability to exercise leadership in the world is limited by its low *per capita* GDP, which means that after providing for the subsistence of the population little is left over for military force and other instruments of power. This is especially true in the modern world, where low per capita income is likely to be associated with especially low capacity in the technology that underlies military power. . . .

A measure of economic strength that can be projected into international power should take some account of per capita income as well as of total income. A suggestive way to do this is to suppose that a certain per capita income must be received for subsistence and that only the national income in excess of that is available for other purposes, including the projection of power. Of course, what constitutes subsistence is a subjective question, and that may turn out to be the heart of the power equation. (I remember a study at the beginning of World War II showing that the Japanese had been

Herbert Stein, "America Is Rich Enough To Be Strong," *The AEI Economist*, February 1988. Reprinted with permission from The American Enterprise Institute for Public Policy Research.

living below the subsistence level for decades. They nevertheless managed to put up a pretty good fight for several years.) If the subsistence level of income in the United States essential for health, morale, and political consensus is equal to per capita GDP, then we obviously have nothing available for defense, foreign aid, and other leadership functions. But to call that an "economic" limit would seem to be stretching the matter. . . .

Suppose we say that what is available for leadership is the GDP in excess of the world average per capita income. Then China drops out of the picture entirely, because China's per capita income is below the world average.

Alternatively we might suppose that the minimum subsistence income is the average per capita income of India. Then China returns to the picture.

The point is that the United States has a higher per capita income than any other country, and when that is added into the equation the relative dominance of the United States increases.

The growth of the U.S. economy has slowed down since 1973. But that has happened in all the major countries except China.

Since 1976 the U.S. economy has grown faster than that of the USSR (or of the Eastern bloc) and of Germany (or of Western Europe as a whole). For the time being we can leave China out of the leadership race because of its low per capita income. So we are left with Japan. If the U.S. and Japanese economies continue to grow at their 1976-1986 rates, Japan's gross national product (GNP) would equal that of the United States in the year 2055. (Japanese per capita GNP would equal that of the United States much earlier, by 2003.) But the excess of the Japanese growth rate over the American has been declining. If the trend of this ratio continues, Japanese GNP will not equal the American until much, much later.

"The combined growth rate of Japan and the European Economic Community has been slightly less than that of the United States."

The combined growth rate of Japan and the European Economic Community has been slightly less than that of the United States in the past ten years. Thus, if all of these growth rates continue, the U.S. share of the combined U.S.-Western Europe-Japan GDP will rise slightly from its present 44 percent.

U.S. GDP is now about 75 percent higher than that of the USSR. If recent trends continue, by the year 2015 the U.S. GDP will be twice as high as that of the Soviet Union.

To project trends of GNP growth for twenty or thirty years is, of course, hazardous. But such projections at least cast doubt on the idea that the United States is now firmly on the declining part of the Kennedy curve.

The currently fashionable notion about the decline of great powers is not only that the U.S. economy is or soon will be in decline but also that the decline results or will result from the country's excessive military burdens. This is a quite incredible idea. For one thing, the slowdown in economic growth that began in 1973 affected all the industrial countries, including Japan, whose military burden was and is trivial. For another thing, in the period of our most rapid growth, from 1948 to 1973, defense expenditures were a much larger fraction of GNP than they have been in the slow-growth period since 1973. In the earlier period, defense expenditures averaged 8.6 percent of GNP. Between 1973 and 1987 they have averaged 5.7 percent. In 1987 they were 6.6 percent.

Ike and the Gipper

In this connection the article by Hodding Carter is ironic. Carter quotes President Eisenhower in 1956 as saying: "But someday there is going to be a man sitting in my present chair who has not been raised in the military services and who will have little understanding of where slashes in their estimates can be made with little or no damage. If that should happen while we still have the state of tension that now exists, I shudder to think of what could happen in this country." To which Hodding Carter adds, "Shudder no more, Ike, meet the Gipper."

But the fact is that the United States devoted a much larger share of the GNP to defense in the Eisenhower period than we have done in the Reagan period. And the Eisenhower administration devoted this larger share to defense even though Soviet military strength was much weaker relative to that of the United States than it is today.

Of course, everything is connected with everything else. Conceivably if the United States spent less on defense and the resources released were used to promote growth, the GNP would grow more rapidly. The lesson people are drawing from the decline-of-empire argument is that the United States should reduce its military spending and would, in fact, be stronger in some international power sense if it did so. But even if a reduction of defense spending would increase GNP growth, the questions would remain whether that would increase America's strength and whether it would be an efficient way of doing so. Suppose that reducing the share of GNP devoted to defense from 7 percent to 6 percent would raise the annual growth rate of GNP from 2.8 percent to 3 percent. (This implies a return to capital of 20 percent, probably not an unreasonably low estimate.) Would the United States be stronger with that much less defense and that much more economic growth? The answer depends upon the nature and imminence of the threat to America's leadership or security. The mere fact, if it is a fact, of a trade-off between defense and growth would not be a case for less defense.

Three Options

But in the American case, at least, that is not the only possible trade-off. One can visualize three options:

	A	B	C
Percent of GNP for defense	7	6	7
Percent of GNP for private consumption	67	67	66
Percent for all other, including investment	26	27	27
GNP growth rate (%)	2.8	3.0	3.0

That is, if we want to devote more of our output to investment in order to have more economic growth in the future, we can achieve that by a slightly lower rate of consumption (option C) rather than by a lower rate of defense spending (option B). No one can say objectively and scientifically that option C is better than option B. If it is extremely important for per capita consumption in the United States to be $12,300 a year rather than $12,116 a year, then option B may be better than option C. Perhaps being a weak country, unable to maintain a position of leadership and security, means that any sacrifice of consumption, from however high a level, is intolerable.

Even if this is not a "scientific" statement, however, I find it hard to believe that keeping consumption in the United States at 67 percent of GNP rather than 66 percent is very important. If we did so and maintained our current growth rate, we would reach any given level of per capita consumption about eight months later than we would otherwise have reached it. That is, we would reach in October the consumption level we would otherwise have reached in February. That hardly seems a delay that should cause the decline of America. We would still have the highest per capita consumption level in the world, probably 20 or 30 percent higher than in Western Europe or Japan.

Defense or Growth

In the U.S. case, at least, to say that the country cannot simultaneously bear the military burdens appropriate to a world leader and maintain a high rate of economic growth means only that we will not sacrifice 1 or 2 percent of per capita consumption.

The choice between defense and growth looks much more difficult than it has been described here because people think of the choice only in terms of

the budget. The defense program seems to be squeezed between irreducible nondefense expenditures in the budget, an immovable ceiling on taxes, and an unbearable deficit. Thus, although cutting consumption by 1½ percent does not seem hard, to get another $50 billion, for example, into the budget for defense seems impossible. That is because we do not look at the budget in a realistic way. We think of the government as an independent entity with an income and needs of its own. But the government and its budget are only instruments by which parts of the national income are allocated to meet some national needs. What is to be allocated to defense comes out of the $4.5 trillion that is the national income, not out of the $1 trillion that is the federal budget. If it is possible, as it surely is, to take another $50 billion out of the $4.5 trillion national income for defense, it is also possible to put another $50 billion into the budget for defense. We would immediately discover that if an urgent need materialized, such as an outbreak of war.

"The most basic fact about the American economy is that it is very rich."

What sometimes seems to set a limit on defense spending below the availability of the real resources is the prospect that more defense spending would require more taxes—something generally regarded as taboo in America. There is a real problem here. The imposition of taxes may create what economists call an "excess burden." That is, to raise $10 billion of taxes may not only transfer $10 billion from the private to the public sector but may also reduce total output because of the negative effect on incentives to work and save. At most, this means that increasing defense spending by, say, $50 billion would require a decrease of consumption not by $50 billion but by $65 billion, because national income would be reduced by $15 billion. This sum is still small in comparison with the massive size of U.S. consumption.

Two Other Points

Two other points should be noted. In terms of the taxes that produce the most severe excess burdens, the high rates of marginal income tax, the United States since the 1986 Revenue Act is better off than at any time since before World War II. That is, because the existing marginal tax rates are lower there is more room for raising additional tax revenue without large negative effects on real output. Moreover, by world standards the United States is a lightly taxed country.

In recent years a new dimension of "weakness" in the economy has come to be regarded as a sign of

America's decline. That is the conversion of America (meaning a statistical aggregation of U.S. individuals and institutions) from being a net creditor to a net debtor of the rest of the world (meaning a statistical aggregation of foreign individuals and institutions). People seem to visualize a situation like the old silent movies where the wicked banker threatens to foreclose on the farmer's mortgage unless the farmer turns over his daughter's hand or his daughter's virtue. But the idea that all the U.S. assets owned abroad could be mobilized and used as a political threat against us by a foreign power—who threatens to sell the assets unless we give up Hawaii, for example—is absurd. So is the idea that the United States would be impressed by such a threat. If foreigners do not want to hold assets in the United States, there will be an adjustment of relative exchange rates, interest rates, and patterns of production that will accommodate them. The situation would be no different if Americans did not want to hold assets in the United States, but that case would be much more severe because Americans hold many more assets in the United States than foreigners do.

The accumulation of net debt to foreigners means that instead of earning a certain amount of income from abroad Americans will, on balance, have to pay a certain amount of income to foreigners. The net investment income of Americans from abroad has just turned negative. But the amounts of income, whether positive or negative, have always been trivial relative to the U.S. national income. At its recent high point, in 1979, the net investment income received from abroad was 1¼ percent of GNP. In the third quarter of 1987, when it turned negative, the net investment income paid to the rest of the world was 2 hundredths of 1 percent of GNP.

The most basic fact about the American economy is that it is very rich. It is not rich enough to do everything, but it is rich enough to do everything important. The only problem is deciding what is important.

Herbert Stein is a senior fellow of the American Enterprise Institute, a public policy research organization.

"The Reagan administration's economic policy . . . has to be judged an enormous success."

Reaganomics Was a Success

Malcolm S. Forbes Jr.

Given the realities of the world and the frailties of human beings, the Reagan administration's economic policy has to be judged an enormous success. The chief achievement of the Reagan presidency is the massive reductions in individual income-tax rates. The benefits that have resulted from those tax reductions outweigh all of the shortcomings and missed opportunities in other areas of the administration's economic policy.

Taxes are not simply a means of raising revenue; they are also a price. The taxes on our income, capital gains, and corporate profits are the price we pay for the privilege of working, the price we pay for being productive, and the price we pay for being innovative and successful. If the price of those things is too high, we get less of them. If the price is lowered, we'll get more of them.

The Kemp-Roth bill of 1981 and the tax reform bill of 1986 reduced individual income-tax rates to levels we hadn't seen in 60 or 70 years. Too many of our policymakers ignore the simple fact that *people* make an economy run—*people* manage companies, not investment tax credits or accelerated depreciation schedules.

To see evidence of that, all we have to do is look at Japan and Britain. Japan's corporate income taxes are about twice as high as ours. By contrast, for almost 30 years Britain had some of the most liberal business depreciation investment incentives and laws in the Western world. Which country has invested more in the past 30 years, Japan or Britain? Which country has had more economic growth? To ask those questions is to answer them. If people have an incentive to get ahead—if they're able to keep enough of what they earn through their labor and innovation—then the economy as a whole benefits,

even if some of the traditional business incentives aren't in force.

The tax reforms of 1981 and 1986 are forcing states to reduce their marginal rates, and they're going to force other industrialized countries to reduce their onerous rates as well. We live in an age of mobility. Brains and money are mobile; they go where the opportunities are. Today the opportunities are more likely to be found in the United States than in most other industrialized nations. Why do we have a capital inflow? It's not because we are big spenders. Nor is it because we have high interest rates—if that were the reason, money would have been going to the Philippines or Zaire. Capital has been coming to this country because there are more opportunities here.

Our tax rate reductions will force other industrialized countries to lower their tax rates not because of anything we might say but because of the sheer pressure of events. In fact, several countries have already begun to compete with each other to do so. The Canadians have made a halting start; the British have said that they will be reducing their rates; the other Europeans are taking small steps; the Japanese are stumbling in that direction. So it's not just the United States that will benefit from our rate reductions; other nations will benefit from them as well—assuming, of course, that Congress doesn't tamper with the tax code again, which is an awfully big assumption. But if the debate goes well, the reduced rates will remain in force, and that's going to have a powerful impact on our economy and those of the Western world.

An Imperfect World

One of the shortcomings in the economic policy of the Reagan years is that the administration did not push privatization, in every area from the Postal Service to Pentagon procurement, as early or as persuasively as it should have. In terms of cutting

Malcolm S. Forbes Jr., "Extending the Reagan Revolution," *Cato Policy Report*, May/June 1988. Reprinted with permission.

back programs or eliminating bad programs and curbing the growth of spending, the administration's record, to be charitable, is very mixed. Its monetary policies have been rather erratic, its approach to Third World debt rather disappointing. The administration doesn't seem to realize that Third World countries are in trouble not because of their indebtedness—which is not much worse than, say, that of Canada or Australia at the turn of the century—but because of being overtaxed, overbureaucratized, and overregulated. . . . But in an imperfect world, the administration can be excused for those shortcomings, grave though they may be, because of what it has done on the tax front.

Economic Hypochondriacs

The success of the administration's tax reforms is evident from the vitriol of its opponents. Certain scholars, policymakers, and politicos seem to be prone to a kind of hypochondria when it comes to looking at the U.S. economy. From what those people write about trade, for example, you would think that America was in the red and Japan was in the black. What gets overlooked is that a trade deficit or surplus is simply a number and that its significance depends upon the particular situation. During the first 100 years of its existence, for example, the United States routinely ran trade deficits. Fortunately, in those days we didn't have an IMF [International Monetary Fund] or a World Bank to tell us that we were doing the wrong thing. As a result of our ignorance, we became a great industrial nation.

Japan ran big trade deficits in the 1950s and the early 1960s. It's very amusing to read what some of our experts wrote about Japan in the 1950s. They didn't write about the emergence of a giant that would humble many of our traditional industries. They wrote about what a hopeless basket case Japan was, and they often cited its large trade deficits. The Japanese were wise enough not to translate that analysis into their language, and we can see what being unaware of it did for them. By contrast, Mexico and Brazil have trade surpluses, but I doubt that even Louisiana or Texas would trade its economy for that of Mexico or Brazil.

Our large trade deficit is a sign of our strength, not our weakness. In the past four or five years our economy has grown more than those of most other nations. We've had enough money and credit to buy more goods and services from them than they have been able to buy from us. If it had not been for the American market, Europe's economy would be even more stagnant than it is, the Third World would be in even worse financial shape, and even Japan would have had considerably lower growth rates.

We've done what a great power is supposed to do: we've carried the rest of the world with us, and we've benefited from doing so as well. If the economies of other nations had grown as much as ours has, if they had done to their tax codes what we have done to ours, and if they had pushed deregulation the way we, at least sometimes, have, they would now be in a position to buy more goods and services from us, and our trade deficit would go the way of the oil shortage.

In short, a trade deficit is neither a good thing nor a bad thing per se; it depends on the circumstances. Look at West Germany. Its economy is weak in many critical respects. Its unemployment rate is high, its job-creation record is unimpressive, and it trails the United States in many areas of technology. But West Germany does have a trade surplus, and it sometimes acts as if it were the Tarzan of the international economy. Because of that one number, the West Germans think they're doing very well.

"The free enterprise system does not appeal to the worst part of human nature but brings out the best in people."

The chief reason for our budget deficit is not that we have had insufficient revenues but that until 1986 there was a rip-roaring increase in government spending. However, our revenues have grown considerably in the past four or five years. Moreover, if you look at what might be called the net government deficit—the combined federal, state, and local deficits and surpluses—as a proportion of GNP [gross national product], you'll find that we've probably done better than the Japanese and not much worse than the West Europeans. That doesn't mean that we've done a good job; it just means that almost everyone else in the world has done as bad a job as we have.

Almost a Balance

In addition, the federal, state, and local governments' combined investment is very high. (Of course, that raises the question of whether governments should be making those kinds of investments. Much of that investing should probably be done by the private sector.) So if you compare the net government deficit with the net government investment, you'll find that our books are almost in balance on an expense level.

The economic hypochondriacs claim that we are a spendthrift nation. You'd never know it from reading what they write, but the net wealth of the American people in real terms is higher today than it's ever been. Our assets have been growing much faster than our liabilities. They also claim that we don't invest enough, but as Alan Reynolds, George Gilder, and others have pointed out, whereas our investment rate has been going up in recent years, those of Japan and Western Europe have been going down.

Contrary to the economic hypochondriacs, manufacturing is the same proportion of our economy today as it was 30 years ago. What we make and how we make it have changed, but our ability to make things has remained basically unchanged. Since the 1982 recession 13½ million jobs have been created, a very large percentage of which have been high-paying jobs. Even though we really misused and abused the economy during the 1970s, in the past 18 years or so we've created over 30 million jobs—more jobs than exist in West Germany, which has the largest economy in Western Europe.

The Intellectual Debate

The administration has failed not in the areas to which the economic hypochondriacs point but in the intellectual debate—the ideological battle. Its opponents have raised the concern that we lack compassion. In our inner cities, we see more illegitimacy, more illiteracy, more crime, more broken families, and more members of a permanent underclass today than ever before. Those conditions, as Charles Murray and others have demonstrated, can be traced directly to social engineering on the state and federal levels. And yet the policies that have had such miserable results remain in effect because they reassure us that we are compassionate. If a law has a "compassionate" purpose, we overlook the fact that the people it was intended to help have actually been hurt by it.

The administration's opponents have been allowed to get away with promoting that way of thinking. It's sort of the equivalent of the days of religious wars, when they would burn you at the stake and you weren't supposed to mind that because it was going to save your soul. The administration has given its opponents a free ride in the intellectual debate.

Unfortunately, even in circles that should know better, people have been buying the notion that the prosperity we've enjoyed during the past few years is the result of selfishness and therefore lacks moral legitimacy. They read about the Ivan Boeskys of the world, and somehow those incidents seem to cast aspersions on our economic gains.

If we're going to succeed in preserving our recent gains and making new gains, we must get across the notion that the free enterprise system does not appeal to the worst part of human nature but brings out the best in people. We must get across the notion that free enterprise gives basic rights to the individual and that letting people develop their talents to the fullest so as to meet the needs and wants of others, whether perceived or unperceived, is moral as well as productive. We must get across the notion that the free enterprise system encourages people to channel their energy into constructive paths instead of the destructive paths that we see being followed in other nations' economies. Some progress has been made in those areas, but not nearly enough.

When people say that we can't let things be determined by the market, we've got to ask, "What is the market?" The market consists of people. When we talk about the discipline of the market, we're talking about individuals deciding whether to buy what's being offered to them. The nation is a democracy in terms of economics as well as politics, but until we get that point across to the public, we're going to be vulnerable to counterattacks by our ideological opponents.

Members of the administration have been weak on attacking mercantilism and beggar-thy-neighbor policies. . . . They know how much damage the Smoot-Hawley tariff did in the 1930s. But they've allowed their opponents to set the terms of the debate, and they've failed to refute the argument that we need protectionism in order to preserve jobs. We have to start pointing out that protectionism is a tax and that a protectionist trade policy would make it a crime for working people to buy a VCR. We have to bring it down to the individual level.

Progress and Change

Change, not stability, is the chief characteristic of the U.S. economy. Progress always involves change, and change is sometimes unsettling. Throughout American history there have been periods that seemed like a hurricane of change, yet the nation has always emerged from those periods the stronger for having weathered the storm. . . .

"When historians look back on this period, they will conclude that the nation's economy and political system had once again confounded the critics."

My feeling is that when historians look back on this period, they will conclude that the nation's economy and political system had once again confounded the critics, the skeptics, and the crepehangers, thus enabling America to reassume its rightful role as the leader and inspiration of the world.

Malcolm S. Forbes Jr. is deputy editor-in-chief of Forbes *magazine.*

"The policies which Mr. Reagan proposed in 1980—for cutting public spending and reducing public interference—have not been fulfilled."

viewpoint 19

Reaganomics Was a Failure

Emma Rothschild

Mr. Reagan's Council of Economic Advisers asserts that the administration's economic program "has become a blueprint" for worldwide growth. Recent US economic growth, they write, "was shaped by government policies explicitly directed toward fostering the inherent dynamism of the private sector." "Our proven market-oriented policies"—the words here are Mr. Reagan's in the accompanying *Economic Report of the President*—"are being adopted in more and more countries around the globe, as they recognize the high cost of big government and the harmful effects of stifling the entrepreneurial spirit."

The Council of Economic Advisers' claim that "market-oriented policies" have been shown to cause (or to "shape") economic recovery has momentous implications. There were about 30 million people unemployed in OECD [Organization for Economic Cooperation and Development] economies in 1987, as there have been every year since 1982. While the United States is not the only country in which employment has boomed during this period, it is the largest and the most conspicuous. It is also conspicuous for the consequences of its public policies, such as in the number of people who are homeless; in the rate of infant mortality (a little higher, in parts of New York City, than in Malaysia, or a little lower than in Guyana); in the rate of deprivation (12.3 million children living in poverty, and 31.3 million people without any health insurance); and in the level of underdevelopment (28,000 people without running water in parts of El Paso, and 53,000 without sewers).

The US economic record has been used to justify right-wing policies around the world. There are international conferences about the "American model," and about growth through the "structural reform" (or repression) of the public sector. In some countries, such as the UK and other high-unemployment economies of the EEC [European Economic Community], Reagan-inspired policies have attracted popular support. In others, such policies have been imposed by international institutions, including the International Monetary Fund; in Mexico, for example, public investment in schools and health clinics has been reduced in response to international pressures, and Sri Lanka has deregulated its food subsidies. "From continent to continent," Mr. Reagan writes in his introduction to the report, "the benefits of privatization and deregulation are becoming appreciated." . . .

What Has Changed

It is urgent to take the argument of the Reagan economists seriously: to see how the US economy has changed since 1981, and to discover what, if anything, that change has to do with the Reagan administration's policies for "fostering" the private sector. The 1988 economic documents of the federal government—the eight-page *Economic Report of the President* and the 359-page *Annual Report* of the Council of Economic Advisers, the Budget of the United States Government, and the National Income and Product Accounts (NIPA) published by the Department of Commerce—provide a fair opportunity to do so. They are the last complete reports of the Reagan period: the funeral oration of the right-wing economic blueprint. They are also, as it turns out, its confutation.

The US economy described in these documents is virtually the opposite of the idyll described by the Republicans. The policies which Mr. Reagan proposed in 1980—for cutting public spending and reducing public interference—have not been fulfilled, or have not had the expected effects. The policies

Emma Rothschild, "The Real Reagan Economy," *The New York Review of Books*, June 30, 1988. Reprinted with permission from *The New York Review of Books*. Copyright © 1988 Nyrev, Inc.

that have succeeded are those rejected in 1980 by the Republicans: fiscal policies that have been consistently in deficit and monetary policies that have been expansive for much of the time since 1983; international borrowing; and increased public spending for health, social security, and the welfare of private services.

Mr. Reagan proposed in 1981 to cut taxes, eliminate the budget deficit, reduce government spending, cut transfer payments (payments made to individuals for welfare and social security), stimulate personal saving, and encourage profits. Personal taxes have instead increased as a share of personal income; profit taxes are now a sharply higher share of profits; the budget deficit has tripled; transfer payments are a higher share of personal income; the savings rate has fallen to its lowest level since 1947; the share of profits in national income has fallen by one third; and the level of profits has suffered its longest slump since the 1930s.

More Dependent

The US economy, after seven years of Republican big government, is even more dependent on social expenditures than it was in 1980. It has become a welfare society for the well-to-do; a conglomeration of semiprivate pension and insurance and medical schemes, clustered at the edges of the public sector and dependent for its survival on public regulation (of schools, insurance, and nursing homes, for example), as well as on public investment, public tax subsidies, and public payments (such as Medicare and Social Security). Government employment, private services such as employment agencies, schools, and health services, and retail trade, together provided 93 percent of all new jobs in the US economy between 1981 and 1986. These are the same low-productivity industries that provided 58 percent of new jobs between 1977 and 1980. More than 32 million Americans work directly for the government, or in the private health, education, and social services.

But the US is a welfare society for only part of the population. There has been a momentous redistribution of income and well-being since the late 1970s: from the poor to the rich, and also from young people and children to the elderly. Some people are inside the little semiprivate welfare states, and other people are far outside. The US has become more snug, in a sense, for the nonpoor, especially for the elderly and for women with good jobs. For the poor and for children, it is something like an underdeveloped country. . . .

The economic indictment of government was set out in the first report of Mr. Reagan's first Council of Economic Advisers, early in 1982. The deterioration of the US economy was said to be the consequence, to a great extent, of federal policies. High taxes were supposed to have reduced

incentives to work and save; transfer payments had reduced employment; and government regulation had increased production costs and reduced productivity. Nothing in the seventh report of Mr. Reagan's counterrevolution supports these views, or suggests that reductions in government's role in the economy have led to economic regeneration.

The Heart of Darkness

Taxes are the heart of darkness of the Reagan philosophy. They were cut during the Republican years, and tax rates have indeed fallen—for all except the very poor—and most sharply for the very rich. But personal taxes actually accounted for exactly the same share of overall personal income—15.08 percent—in 1987 as in 1980. The average share was 14.82 percent in the Reagan years from 1981 to 1987, and 14.67 percent in the Carter years from 1977 to 1980. There was a more pronounced increase in corporate taxes. Liability for taxes on profits increased as a share of before-tax profits from 35.8 percent in 1980 to 50.1 percent in 1987; the average share was 41.1 between 1981 and 1987, up from 35.5 percent between 1977 and 1980.

It is difficult, in these conditions, to think of a fair test of the effects of tax cuts on economic recovery. The Reagan economic philosophers would no doubt argue that it is tax rates that are the principal culprit in inhibiting economic activity, particularly taxes on the rich. As they explain in their 1984 report, "Some taxes are more harmful than others. . . . Taxes do more harm when levied on individuals or activities that are more responsive to tax rules." The reduction in rich (and thereby "responsive") people's taxes might thus be responsible for fostering markets.

"Nothing . . . suggests that reductions in government's role in the economy have led to economic regeneration."

The specific effects that were anticipated in the 1982 report are hardly helpful, all the same. Tax cuts were then expected to increase incentives for people to join the labor force, and to work extra hours. But the labor force, and the labor force participation rate, instead grew more slowly between 1981 and 1987 than between 1970 and 1980. Hours worked per employee have also declined since 1981. There are many demographic and other factors to explain these tendencies, for which the Reagan administration's tax theory could in principle be adjusted. But the theory is beginning to look distinctly thin: a noncut in taxes has produced a nonincrease in effort. . . .

The Reagan economists can now suggest that the reduction in the "role of government" has "shaped" a "market-oriented" economic recovery. But the evidence in the *Report* turns out, once again, to be less than helpful.

One indicator of the government's "role" in the economy is the extent of the government deficit, or the difference between what governments spend and what they receive. This old and trusted indicator stood at $10.6 billion, on average (or −0.4 percent of GNP [gross national product]) between 1977 and 1980, and at $108.9 billion (−2.8 percent of GNP) between 1981 and 1987. The explanation for the rise is an increase in government spending, and not a reduction in taxes. Government receipts have increased by 0.6 percent of GNP from the earlier to the later period. Defense spending, meanwhile, accounted for less than half of the increase in spending—1.2 percent of GNP—while nondefense government spending increased by 1.8 percent of GNP.

Defense Spending

Defense spending, after seven years of misconceived military expansion, still accounts for less than 30 percent of total federal government spending. Overall government spending increased as a share of GNP from 31.5 percent between 1977 and 1980 to 34.6 percent between 1981 and 1987; and within the Reagan-recovery period from 33 percent in 1981 to 35 percent in 1987. The increase remains when defense is excluded from total spending, and when the government's role in the economy is defined as government "consumption" (or purchase of goods and services). The sternest measure of government spending that is held to threaten the market—the compensation of nondefense government employees as a share of GNP—increased from 7.9 percent in 1981 to 8.1 percent in 1987.

Even within the "private" sector, the Reagan years have favored the economic activities that are most dependent on government. National output may be divided into the product of three sectors, business enterprise, nonprofit institutions, and government. Business is much the largest of the three. But its relative position has decreased since 1981, while that of government has increased slightly, and that of the nonprofit sector has increased most. Nonprofit institutions now constitute an "industry" with an output somewhat larger than that of the motor vehicles and electric and electronic equipment industries combined, and they employ about eight million people, whether in hospitals, museums, universities, or day-care centers, for example. They mostly supply health, education, and social services: the same services in which business enterprise has flourished during the Reagan years. . . .

The insidious role of government, according to Mr. Reagan's first *Economic Report*, was "far deeper and broader than even the growing burden of spending and taxing would suggest." The government's "vast web of regulations" had adversely affected productivity. But the growth of Federal regulation was already slowing down, at least "as suggested by a 27 percent decline in the number of pages in the *Federal Register*." This would lead, it was anticipated, to faster growth in productivity: "Regulatory reform will make its greatest impact in raising productivity and reducing costs."

The authors of the 1988 report claim that there has been an "accelerated growth of productivity" since 1981 and that it is the result of "a general approach to policy that emphasizes reliance on the private sector." Mr. Reagan himself points to the worldwide appreciation for the benefits of deregulation. But the Reagan economists provide no convincing evidence of a causal relationship between growth of productivity and deregulation. The improvement of productivity through deregulation is still—after seven years of effort by the "Task Force on Regulatory Relief" and its chairman Mr. Bush—a matter for "the years ahead."

"The Reagan economists provide no convincing evidence of a causal relationship between growth of productivity and deregulation."

The Reagan economists were probably right to attribute part of the decline in growth of productivity in the 1970s to government policies, especially those having to do with safety and the environment. The policies reflected a relatively sudden change in people's preferences, or in their "judgements about the value" of the physical environment. These judgements were embodied in increased regulation during the Seventies. But the "problem" is one of preferences more than of regulations. The mining industry, for example, produces less pollution and has fewer accidents than it did during the 1950s. Most of the administration's "reforms" have in any case been concerned with regulations that are far older than the environmental legislation of the 1970s.

The "accelerated growth of productivity" is itself distinctly modest. Output per hour increased by 1.6 percent per year between 1981 and 1987, compared to an average of 2.7 percent per year between 1950 and 1970, and 1.2 percent per year between 1970 and 1980. The US still has among the lowest rates of growth of productivity of any OECD country. The most plausible explanation for the slight improvement in the 1980s has nothing to do with the Reagan reforms; it is a matter, rather, of the rapid increase in business investment during the expansion of the Carter period.

The only specific argument in the report about recovery and deregulation, that "deregulation substantially improved productivity and efficiency in the transportation sector," is not at all convincing. The deregulation of transport was largely an achievement of the Carter administration—in the Airline Deregulation Act of 1978, for example, to which the report devotes several pages—and it has had various good effects, such as some reductions in the price of air tickets. These good effects do not include increases in productivity. The "product" of the transport industry—the value of the air tickets and freight services it sells, less the value of the fuel and advertisements it buys—has increased more slowly than its employment. Output per hour in transportation, according to Labor Department statistics used in the Report, increased by 2.1 percent per year from 1950 to 1970, and by 2.6 percent per year from 1970 to 1978: it fell by 0.8 percent per year from 1978 to 1986.

The deregulation of the financial industries was even less helpful to the Reagan economists' view that the rise in productivity resulted from a decline of the government's role. Employment in financial services has boomed during the recent expansion, notably in credit agencies and security brokers. But the output produced per person in financial industries—the value of brokerage services sold, for example, less costs for messengers and supplies—was lower in 1986 than in 1980. It was lower, even, than in 1950. . . .

The Spiritual View

Mr. Reagan and his advisers often allude to a spiritual view of economic recovery. The "spirit" of enterprise was in 1980 "still there, ready to blaze into life." The sources (or "vital forces") of economic growth were essentially psychological: "creativity and ambition," or "the motivation and incentive of our people." The first object of the new economic policy was therefore to "rekindle the Nation's entrepreneurial instincts." Its instruments were political as well as economic reform, and in particular the reduction of government.

This view of recovery is evidently convenient for Republican economists. Economic growth, they suggest, can be explained by noneconomic forces. The blueprint for market-oriented resurgence is no longer dependent on such confining economic indicators as taxes, transfers, savings, and the extent of government. There is no reason, on such a view, that the Reagan policies must succeed in order to be successful. The declaration of an intention to reduce government or increase profits may improve the national spirit, even though the policies do not then succeed. The fortunes of the very rich and the very poor may rekindle the instincts of everyone:

> In society the extreme parts could not be diminished beyond a certain degree without lessening that animated exertion throughout the middle parts. . . . If no man could hope to rise or fear to fall, in society, if industry did not bring with it its reward and idleness its punishment, the middle parts would not certainly be what they are now.

This was Malthus's view of the invigorating psychological effects of inequality, and it has not really been out of fashion since the 1790s; it is an argument, of sorts, for spiritual recovery.

"Investment accounted for a much lower share of national product during the Reagan administration than in the preceding years."

No effort has been made here to describe the psychological view of economic recovery. This is unjust, no doubt. But there are limits to the spiritual hypothesis. The most obvious economic role for euphoria is to explain otherwise obscure increases in investment. People are thought to be exhilarated because of increases in profits or reductions in taxes, and they therefore exert themselves to invest.

There is no need, in the 1980s, for such spiritual explanations, because there has been no increase in investment. Investment accounted for a much lower share of national product during the Reagan administration than in the preceding years. Gross private domestic investment amounted to 17.5 percent of GNP, on average, between 1977 and 1980, and 15.9 percent between 1981 and 1987. The fall in net investment (as a share of NNP [net national product]) was even sharper: from 7.8 percent to 5.2 percent.

Even the "surge" in profits after 1981 cannot explain economic growth and entrepreneurial euphoria—because there has been no surge in profits. The share of profits in national income has instead plummeted in the Reagan period: from 12.1 percent, on average, between 1977 and 1980 to 7.5 percent on average between 1981 and 1987. These are figures for profits before tax and before adjustments for capital consumption allowances. The plunge has been even more serious for after-tax profits. Corporation taxes have increased, as already noted, and after-tax profits have fallen from 7.8 percent of national income between 1977 and 1980 to only 4.5 percent between 1981 and 1987. The Reagan administration has increased government spending, increased transfer payments, increased the Federal debt, and invented unprecedented disincentives to private saving; it has also presided over the most sustained fall in profits since the 1930s.

Emma Rothschild is a research fellow at Kings College of Cambridge University in England.

"It would have been far better for all concerned had S&Ls stuck to their knitting and had government continued to supervise them."

Deregulation Caused the Thrift Crisis

Kevin Kelly and Robert Kuttner

Editor's note: This viewpoint is in two parts. Part I is by Kevin Kelly. Part II is by Robert Kuttner.

I

Ed McBirney had a reputation as a party animal. For Halloween 1984 the owner of Dallas-based Sunbelt Savings and Loan Association dressed as a king and offered guests their choice of lion, pheasant or antelope meat. McBirney, pulling in a six-figure income, had transformed Sunbelt into a $1.3-billion institution through real estate speculation. The savings and loan (thrift) was so famous for outgunning the competition that it became known as "Gunbelt."

Today McBirney and hundreds of other thrift owners like him are out of business. But these financial wildcatters left behind a ravaged industry. There are 3,000 thrifts in the U.S. About 1,000 of them are losing money—a total of $7 billion in 1988. More than half the money-losers—like Sunbelt—are insolvent. Their loans are worthless and many of them possess real estate with little or no value.

Close the Thrifts

Most experts think these thrifts—based mainly in California, Florida, Georgia and Texas—should be closed. But there's a catch: paying off their depositors, who are protected by federal insurance, could cost $100 billion. Articulating a growing consensus on Capitol Hill, House Banking Committee member Rep. Henry Gonzalez (D-TX) says, "A taxpayer bailout is the only option I see."

Given the escalating nature of the crisis, the Bush administration . . . moved against the thrift industry within its first 100 days. Congress is now worried the crisis could undermine confidence in the

Kevin Kelly, "Who'll Save the Savings and Loans?" *In These Times*, November 9-15, 1988. Reprinted with permission. Robert Kuttner, "'It's a Wonderful Life': The Sad Sequel," *The Washington Post National Weekly Edition*, October 17-23, 1988. © The Washington Post. Reprinted with permission.

financial system, triggering a dollar run that those papering over the budget deficit can least afford.

Moreover, many now admit the Federal Savings and Loan Insurance Corporation (FSLIC) hasn't the resources or the staff to manage the crisis. . . . It . . . flailed away at its Southwest Plan [in summer 1988], merging sick thrifts and trying to sell others. In late summer 1988 it put together several deals, including one that turned over the nation's largest and sickest thrift to billionaire corporate-raider Robert M. Bass.

That sale frightened many industry watchers who fear financiers like Bass will simply use federally insured deposits in risky takeover deals. "That's what got us in this problem in the first place," says one thrift owner. . . .

Roots of the Crisis

The thrift industry hasn't always been so controversial. Back in the '40s it started out at the local level, with institutions making mortgage loans to help people buy houses. But with its role usurped by the growth of mortgage-backed securities and new lending institutions, including General Motors, thrifts drifted into an identity crisis.

That identity crisis spawned a fiscal crisis. The industry was already starting to skid in the late '70s, when regulations restricted the interest thrifts could pay depositors and higher-yield, money-market funds became available. In 1980 the federal government eased the interest-rate cap, but then the interest thrifts paid depositors failed to keep pace with interest earned on loans. A year later thrifts were paying depositors an average of 11 percent, while getting only 10 percent on 30-year, fixed-rate mortgages.

In 1982 Congress decided to help the ailing industry by deregulating it. The Garn-St. Germain Act allowed thrifts to branch out into new lending territories, including both real estate and business loans. This freedom attracted a new breed of thrift owner—high-rollers like McBirney, who saw an opportunity to make big money using federally insured cash to buy risk-laden, high-yield assets.

These mavericks began searching for deposits to bankroll their adventures. Money brokers arose to service them, bringing new funds in the form of $100,000 certificates of deposit. These "jumbo CDs," which earned interest at higher than the prevailing rate, became known as "hot money." On any given day institutional and individual investors shopped the market, seeking the highest rates. Limiting each deposit to $100,000 gave investors federal protection.

"These investors didn't care what the thrift did with their money," says one industry analyst, "because they knew whatever happened, the money was insured."

No Rules but Their Own

With ready cash and new powers, many thrifts went wild. Sunbelt grew 5,200 percent over three years making loans in the volatile Dallas real estate market. Butterfield Savings and Loan in Santa Ana, Calif., quintupled its assets in 1983 to $492 million. It bought fast-food franchises and lost heavily. Sunrise Savings and Loan in Boynton Beach, Fla., grew from $5 million to $1.5 billion in assets between 1980 and 1985, often investing in speculative real estate deals.

These thrift entrepreneurs lived by their own rules. They closed deals with handshakes, often doing no research into the value of the land or the company they were lending on. Number-crunching bored them. Instead they organized "land flips," successive sales of a land parcel that inflated the value and produced good income for each seller in the chain of deals.

By 1985 the Federal Home Loan Bank Board (FHLBB), which oversees the thrift industry, sputtered into action. Then-Chair Edwin Gray recognized that thrifts were loaning far too much on speculative projects. But his attempts to end this were foiled. The Reagan administration, dedicated to deregulation, refused to give Gray more money to hire bank examiners.

Moreover, influential members of Congress who received big donations from thrift owners pressed the FHLBB to lay off their favorite thrifts. House Speaker Jim Wright (D-TX) raised $240,000 from thrifts for his 1986 campaign, 20 percent of his total war chest. Not surprisingly, Wright intervened for thrift owners on several occasions. Meanwhile, industry lobbyists thwarted any attempts to re-regulate the industry.

But the collapse of oil prices in 1985 set off a chain reaction, leading to the collapse of real estate values in the Southwest. Suddenly hundreds of thrifts were insolvent.

In 1986 the FSLIC ran out of money, but the games continued. Fearing new cash would be used to liquidate insolvent thrifts, the industry lobbied hard to limit FSLIC's recapitalization. During the summer of 1987 Congress responded, authorizing FSLIC to issue a paltry $10.8 billion in bonds.

So far the FHLBB has committed $21 billion in its various rescue efforts—that's $11 billion more than its budget. FHLBB Chair M. Danny Wall argues that he'll make up the difference by charging higher insurance premiums, but any such move would likely initiate a revolt from the owners of healthy thrifts, who are already burdened by excessive premiums.

Taxpayers Bear Burden

That leaves the problem to the taxpayers. FSLIC would use the $100 billion to bail out the insolvent thrifts and pay off their depositors. Many industry experts, like Virginia-based consultant Bert Ely, expect the rest of the thrifts to be rechartered as banks.

"America doesn't need a housing finance industry anymore," he says.

Moreover, as banks, the former thrifts would face higher capital requirements and tougher supervision from the Federal Deposit Insurance Corporation.

Congress is also seriously looking at reforming deposit insurance. Rather than insuring accounts to $100,000, some suggest a figure like $40,000. "This would force those who want to take advantage of high CD rates to accept the risk of their investment," says one former thrift owner.

"Many share the blame for the crisis. Congress held up regulatory action and the Reagan administration thoughtlessly deregulated."

Undoubtedly, many share the blame for the crisis. Congress held up regulatory action and the Reagan administration thoughtlessly deregulated. Both encouraged an easy-money, casino mentality among thrift owners just as they did among stockbrokers.

But the industry itself, with worn-out purpose, should shoulder much of the blame. It tolerated and encouraged bad business practices, falling victim to the greed that has so dominated '80s corporate culture.

II

Economic deregulation has enjoyed a spectacular vogue during the Reagan years. But anybody who still has illusions about its virtues should consider the nation's savings-and-loan industry.

S&Ls—also known as "thrift" institutions—began as nonprofit associations designed to provide small depositors a safe place to accumulate savings and obtain mortgage loans. The virtuous savings and loan versus the greedy commercial bank was idealized in the Jimmy Stewart movie "It's a Wonderful Life." Today the thrift industry has become the worst banking calamity since the Great Depression. Thirty percent of the industry is running in the red; hundreds of S&Ls have been closed. Experts are divided over whether the ultimate taxpayer cost will be $40 billion to $50 billion, or $80 to $100 billion. The Federal Home Loan Bank Board, the industry's regulator (after a fashion), is hastily arranging fire sales of ailing S&Ls, in hopes of getting some of the liability off the government's books.

How could this happen? For nearly half a century, savings institutions were pillars of financial stability. The New Deal gave the thrift industry and home ownership a boost by providing deposit insurance, as well as a Federal National Mortgage Association to buy up mortgages that S&Ls wrote and to pump in new funds.

Stern Policing

But since government was guaranteeing the money, government was necessarily a stern policeman. Regulations limited the interest thrift institutions (and banks) could pay savers, to keep rates predictable and low. And the government sharply restricted speculation by S&Ls. The approach was conservative with a small c.

In the 1970s, inflation struck. S&Ls found themselves stuck with 30-year, 7 percent mortgages, while they had to pay depositors 10 percent and 12 percent to attract savings. Congress delayed permitting thrifts to issue variable-rate mortgages as a way for them to share the risk of inflation with borrowers. The first wave of deregulation, permitting banks and money-market mutual funds to compete head to head with S&Ls, worsened the squeeze. But despite losses, as late as 1980 the industry was essentially solvent.

In the 1980s, the Reagan administration decided to turn loose S&Ls as entrepreneurs—only it neglected to cancel the deposit insurance. A new breed of entrepreneur displaced the Jimmy Stewart types, attracted by the gospel of deregulation. Several states, led by California and Texas, permitted S&Ls to become full-blown speculators, using federally insured deposits.

A savings and loan could invest as much as 100 percent of the depositors' money in real-estate venture, fast-food franchises, oil wells, anything that looked like a money-maker. If the investment panned out, the entrepreneur got rich; if it failed, Uncle Sam picked up the tab. This was too good to be true.

In 1982 the Reagan administration permitted S&Ls to use Wall Street money brokers to collect unlimited funds in short-term deposits, repealing a previous 5 percent limit on such funds. This meant that a tiny savings association, with a few hundred thousand dollars of capital, could offer half a point interest above what the market was paying and become a billion-dollar player overnight. Its potential losses were unlimited.

In mid-1983 a conservative Republican, Edwin Gray, was named chairman of the Federal Home Loan Bank Board. Gray had been policy director of the White House staff; he had worked for Ronald Reagan since 1966. But he also had been in the savings-and-loan business himself, and he was appalled at what he saw.

Tighter Accounting Rules

Gray tried to stop the hot money coming from money brokers. He wrote regulations limiting S&Ls' ability to invest in speculative deals. He sought to tighten accounting rules, to force thrifts to be adequately capitalized. He also asked the Office of Management and Budget for additional bank examiners. At the time, the starting salary of a bank examiner was $14,000, and a quarter of the examining force was quitting every year.

Gray quickly found himself damned as a re-regulator. The additional examiners were denied. The White House blocked several of his proposals. Congressional allies of the S&L industry blocked others. Eventually, only after irrevocable damage had been done, did the mood, and the policies, toughen.

"There was a mentality in those days that deregulation would solve everything," says Gray, who resigned [in] 1987. "Nobody seemed to understand that thrift institutions were not free-market institutions because they were backed by the full faith and credit of the United States."

"Only after irrevocable damage had been done, did the mood, and the policies, toughen."

There is nothing conservative about letting speculators run wild with federally insured money. Taking in deposits and making home-mortgage loans is essentially a pretty simple business. It would have been far better for all concerned had S&Ls stuck to their knitting and had government continued to supervise them. That basic economics lesson will cost us upwards of $50 billion.

Kevin Kelly is a Dallas journalist who writes about business issues. Robert Kuttner is economics editor for The New Republic.

Government Regulation Caused the Thrift Crisis

Catherine England

The financial services sector facilitates the operation of the rest of the economy by performing two basic functions. One is that financial firms move money to the highest valued use by gathering information and acting as intermediaries between savers and borrowers. The other is that financial institutions help individuals spread risk by pooling their resources.

To be able to perform these functions, and thereby help promote broadly based economic growth, the financial services sector needs to be both stable and efficient. Unfortunately, though, current government policies make it difficult to achieve these objectives. Federal laws and regulations applied to banks, savings and loan associations, insurance companies, securities firms, and the real estate markets introduce instability, and many government practices encourage excessive risk taking. Financial institutions are limited in their ability to diversify their portfolios, are kept from adapting to changing market conditions, and are constrained in their ability to efficiently serve consumer and business markets.

These are serious charges. They are meant to be. To correct existing problems, it is necessary to understand how current policies are counterproductive vis-a-vis their stated goals.

Government Failures

It is widely accepted that the banking industry is inherently unstable. Because bankers hold only a portion of their deposits as liquid reserves and use those deposits to fund illiquid loans, it is argued that an unregulated banking system would be exposed to periodic panics and collapses that could disrupt the broader economy.

This line of reasoning is disturbing for those who believe that markets generally behave rationally. In the several centuries that bankers have offered their services, why has no superior system developed? It is difficult to believe that an economic function as important as banking can be carried out only through inherently unstable institutions.

An alternative to the generally accepted market failure view deserves further attention. Although many scholars have described how specific government policies have undermined the stability of the banking system, few have asked more basic questions. For example, has a history of government intervention in monetary and banking arrangements prevented the market from developing a superior financial system? And has the observed instability been caused by government policies rather than by an inherent flaw in the market? A strong case can be made that the widely identified problems in the banking industry can be more accurately attributed to policy failures rather than to market failures.

To explore this case, three government failures are discussed here: (1) the problems with federal deposit insurance, (2) the government's misdirected failure resolution policies, and (3) the problems introduced by an inflexible regulatory apparatus.

Federal deposit insurance was introduced to add stability to the banking system. Because depositors are presumed to be unable to differentiate healthy banks from unsound ones, federal guarantees were designed to protect banks from unfounded panic-driven withdrawals by depositors and to give banking regulators an opportunity to close insolvent banks or thrift institutions in an orderly manner. Given the economic chaos of the 1930s, the arguments made by proponents of federal deposit insurance carried considerable weight, especially as the program offered a means of doing something tangible to address the depression-era banking crisis. . . .

Catherine England, "A Market Approach to the Savings and Loan Crisis." *An American Vision: Policies for the '90s.* Edward H. Crane and David Boaz, eds. Washington, DC: The Cato Institute, 1989. Reprinted with permission.

Critics argued that federal deposit insurance would lead depositors to become indifferent about the relative stability of insured banks. In a brief filed with the House Committee on Banking and Currency, the American Bankers Association described the consequences of introducing federal guarantees: "[The deposit guaranty plan] proposes to place the reckless and speculative banks on the same level with the best managed and the most conservative, which will lead to competition calculated to drag all of them down to the least meritorious." Thus, it was recognized as early as 1932 that removing depositors as a source of market discipline would free more aggressive bank managers to pursue additional risks in a search for higher profits, a phenomenon we now call moral hazard.

These early criticisms of federal deposit guarantees were prescient. It has become increasingly apparent that few federally insured depositors care how bank and thrift managers invest their funds. Indeed, depositor apathy has progressed to the point of so-called rate chasing. Frequently, individuals holding accounts in failed S&Ls have taken their federal deposit insurance checks and deposited them with whatever institution is then paying the highest rate on deposits—without asking any questions about the financial health of their new thrift, and confident in the knowledge that the government guarantees not only principal but also accrued interest. And although federal regulation is supposed to replace depositor oversight, it is apparent that federal examiners who visit a bank twice a year are no match for innovative depository managers searching for new ways to enhance the profitability of their institutions. . . .

"Centralized supervision is inadequate to replace depositor discipline."

The presence of federal deposit insurance has reduced the stability of the banking industry by alleviating depository managers of the need to compete for customers on the basis of sound banking practices and financial health. The system designed to eliminate unfounded panics has created an environment in which individuals knowingly place large sums of money in insolvent institutions to earn a slightly higher return on their deposits. Depositors are no longer running from unsound institutions; in many cases they are running to them. This places the entire supervisory burden on federal examiners. By its nature, however, centralized supervision is inadequate to replace depositor discipline. . . .

By failing to deal promptly with insolvent depositories or by providing financial assistance to failing institutions, regulators reinforce depositors' lack of concern about the financial health of their banks and S&Ls, and federal authorities send depository managers a message that undermines the impact of threats of regulatory action directed at inappropriate behavior. Rather than taking steps, as private insurers do, to alleviate the moral hazard problem, the federal guarantors have pursued actions that compound the problem.

Penalizes Healthy Institutions

The failure on the part of federal regulators to allow the financial market to rid itself of dead wood also penalizes healthy institutions. Several hundred insolvent S&Ls continue to gather deposits and make loans. Many other uneconomic banks and thrifts have received regulators' attention only to be supported through government-sponsored bailouts and below-market loans. These practices have skewed the competitive environment in a way that has encouraged even conservatively managed banks and thrifts to move toward portfolios embodying more risk.

The managers and owners of insolvent or near-insolvent depository institutions focus on short-term survival. They bid up interest rates paid on deposits and force down interest rates charged for loans as they seek to cover near-term cash commitments and pursue riskier investments in the hope of a quick killing that will recapitalize their ailing institutions. Healthier depositories, forced to compete with these zombies, must often match, or at least approach, the uneconomic rates set by the riskiest portion of the industry. . . .

We no longer need 30,000 separately capitalized and managed depository institutions, if we ever did. Weaker firms should be leaving the industry, and the survivors should be consolidating and reorganizing their operations to reduce costs and more effectively serve customers. Unfortunately, regulatory practices are slowing this process by keeping insolvent depositories in operation and imposing legal barriers on institutions attempting to restructure their operations. Relief for the overcrowded banking industry has been delayed, and profit margins for the industry have been reduced.

The federal government's deposit insurance and closure policies are rapidly creating a system where indiscriminate risk taking is rewarded while prudence is discouraged. Furthermore, market forces attempting to rid the industry of unneeded capacity are being counteracted by federal policies. For financial institutions, this is a recipe for disaster. If these policies are not corrected, a taxpayer bailout is certain, and eventual nationalization cannot be ruled out.

Although the deposit insurance and closure systems of the federal government are the most important sources of government failure, they are only part of the problem. The entire regulatory apparatus, anchored as it is in a 1930s view of banking and financial markets, has contributed to the difficulties facing the U.S. financial system.

The most egregious example of regulatory restrictions introducing risk is the long-standing prohibition against nationwide branching. U.S. banking law has made it difficult for banks to diversify either the sources of their deposits or their loan portfolios, and consequently, these constraints have created a history of recurring local and regional banking crises. The regional difficulties apparent today among "energy" banks and "farm" banks stem from the concentrated nature of their loan portfolios and are only the most recent example of this self-inflicted wound.

Similarly, the beginnings of the thrift industry crisis can be found in regulations closely defining the economic role of thrifts and restricting their activities to fit that part. S&Ls historically have been required to invest the lion's share of their portfolios in long-term, locally generated, fixed-rate home mortgages, and these loans have been funded by collecting short-term savings deposits. When interest rates began to rise rapidly during the early 1980s, thrift managers found their cost of funds rising while the returns on their loan portfolios remained flat. Equity capital was rapidly absorbed, and an increasing number of savings and loans became insolvent.

Covering Up Failure

The federal regulators either would not or could not close the growing number of insolvent savings and loans in a timely manner. Attempting to hide this regulatory failure, federal authorities lowered the minimum acceptable amount of capital and redefined the accounting rules to allow S&Ls to artificially inflate their reported capital accounts. Federal deposit insurance protected these decapitalized institutions from runs by their depositors. Owners and managers of insolvent thrifts rightly concluded they had little to lose in pursuing greater risks that promised large returns. Success could mean a newly recapitalized institution—and failure would only mean a bigger bill for the Federal Savings and Loan Insurance Corporation (FSLIC).

While not as important to date, regulations restricting the range of activities in which commercial banks may engage also have become increasingly binding. The restrictions that prevent commercial banks from offering investment banking services have been of particular concern. The best credit risks have been lost to the commercial paper and noninvestment-grade bond markets, while margins between interest rates charged and the costs of banks' funds have been reduced, even for less-creditworthy customers. Many bankers have responded by taking on more credit risk and by pursuing new fee-for-service and off-balance-sheet activities in their attempt to replace lost revenue.

"It is difficult if not impossible for regulatory systems to anticipate and accommodate change."

The current regulatory system was written using a strictly defined view of the proper business of banks, thrifts, securities firms, and insurance companies. This model might have been appropriate to the mid-1930s, but it is not as suitable today. Just as the communications and transportation industries have evolved with an array of products and services unforeseen 50 years ago, the financial services industry must also be allowed to progress. The current regulatory structure, with its built-in definitions and expectations about the economic role that different financial firms can and should play, cannot accommodate widespread change in financial products and services. The fact that banks of the 1930s funded illiquid loans with potentially volatile deposits does not mean banks would necessarily operate in the same way today. If banks were liberated from the mold established by long-standing regulatory practices, new methods for providing secure liquid-deposit instruments and meeting the credit needs of individuals, as well as small and mid-sized companies, would be more likely to develop. That brings us to the final criticism.

Even allowing for the possibility of banking-law revisions, extensive regulation is destabilizing because it is inflexible. Regardless of how well-intentioned or well-thought-out the original regulatory system, and despite the appointment of intelligent, diligent administrators, government-sponsored regulatory structures simply cannot keep pace with a changing marketplace.

Resisting Change

It is difficult if not impossible for regulatory systems to anticipate and accommodate change. They are based on the world as we know it, not as it may become. Furthermore, political decisionmakers balancing the claims of competing interest groups often are rewarded for resisting the emergence of new technologies and new competitors. When politicians do act, cost-effective service to consumers and long-term stability frequently take a back seat to protecting the profits of a well-identified producers' group and delaying problems until after the next election. Thus, as market-driven events unfold, regulatory constraints (even those originally designed to increase the industry's profitability) can become binding restrictions that encumber the ability of financial institutions to compete effectively and survive. . . .

The federal government's regulatory attitudes toward banks and other financial institutions have caused more problems than they have solved in the past half-century. Although federal deposit insurance is seen by some as the glue holding the thrift industry together, it is more accurately pictured as a sticky spider's web that has brought the nation's S&Ls (and many banks) to the precipice. Furthermore, the moral hazard that is the narcotic of federal deposit guarantees has been enhanced by closure policies that first delay dealing with inadequately capitalized institutions and then provide bailouts or below-market loans when forced to respond to an insolvent depository. Finally, the federal government's regulatory policies have failed because decisionmakers have responded to political considerations rather than economic and market concerns in debates over possible reform. The evolution of U.S. financial markets has thus been stifled by the weight of 50-year-old definitions and attitudes concerning the acceptable role for each financial institution.

It is time to move forward. It is time to establish government policies that promote efficiency and stability among our financial institutions. Four broad policy initiatives are required:

1. Resolve the thrift industry crisis as quickly as possible, in order to minimize the expenditure of taxpayer funds.
2. Move to reduce dependence on federal deposit insurance and emphasize market discipline.
3. Remove existing barriers to interstate branching.
4. Remove existing ownership and affiliate restrictions applied to banks and other financial institutions.

Catherine England is director of regulatory studies of the Cato Institute in Washington, DC.

"Thrift executives, lobbyists, lawmakers, and regulators were locked into a relationship so cozy that it was hard to tell... where the industry ends and the government begins."

viewpoint **22**

Corruption Caused the Thrift Crisis

Kathleen Day

Forget the lavish lifestyle of savings and loan executives in Texas and California—the trips to Europe in search of a good chef, the leather toilet seats, the $100 tips to waitresses in coffee shops. Forget the party where an officer at a now-failed S&L donned the costume of a king and served lion and antelope meat to guests. And forget the well-publicized attempts by congressmen—Jim Wright, Don Riegle, Fernand St Germain, Alan Cranston—to keep regulators from cracking down on S&Ls that spent their depositors' money this mindlessly.

These are just symptoms of a deeper regulatory failure during the 1980s, a failure that allowed the savings and loan crisis to grow in a few years from a problem of several billion dollars to one that will cost the public at least $157 billion over the next ten years and $230 billion over the next 30. By the time scores of S&L executives had started living like Leona Helmsley, and Wright and Riegle had started doing favors for them, the system was already hopelessly messed up. Thrift executives, lobbyists, lawmakers, and regulators were locked into a relationship so cozy that it was hard to tell (and it still is) where the industry ends and the government begins. Given the mutual interest most of these people had in keeping the S&L problem quiet, there was little chance that it would be checked before it approached apocalyptic proportions.

Incompetence and Corruption

Space doesn't permit a detailed accounting of the sins of all these people. This is a shame, since so many of them—Republicans and Democrats alike—have such colorful histories of incompetence and corruption. Still, there's plenty to be learned by recounting the records of the cream of the crop—the dozen or so people who are most spectacularly

Kathleen Day, "When Hell Sleazes Over," *The New Republic*, March 20, 1989. Reprinted by permission of THE NEW REPUBLIC, © 1989, The New Republic, Inc.

culpable. There's therapeutic value in this, too; if we are really going to be paying for this fiasco for decades, it will be helpful to have a few handy receptacles for our wrath. Let's start at the beginning.

Frank Capra. Capra, unlike all the other people on the blame list, made only a slight contribution to the S&L crisis and an entirely innocent one. He merely created the film *It's a Wonderful Life*, in which Jimmy Stewart played the affable head of a savings and loan, a man motivated mainly by a desire to help his neighbors secure a home. The film both reflected and reinforced the apple-pie image of S&Ls that lobbyists have skillfully exploited to shield their industry from the sort of congressional and public scrutiny that could have exposed the S&L crisis in an earlier, less expensive phase.

Back when the movie was made, S&Ls were still devoted to encouraging homebuying in straightforward fashion. They matched customers who wanted to save long-term with homebuyers who wanted to borrow long-term. For performing this service, the thrifts were rewarded with a variety of subsidies. They occupied a cozy, government-controlled environment. There was a cap on the interest that S&Ls (and banks) could pay, the theory being that interest-rate wars were destabilizing. For years S&L executives lived by the 3-6-3 rule. Pay three percent for deposits. Lend the money to homebuyers at six percent. Play golf at three.

Today's S&L problems started in the late 1970s. Financial markets became more sophisticated as technology provided a wider array of investment instruments, such as mutual funds and money market funds. As stagflation hit the economy, interest rates rose, and these instruments started offering higher yields; banks and S&Ls saw depositors withdraw funds in the billions. Responding to cries for help, Congress lifted interest caps in 1980 so that S&Ls and banks could lure back

america's economy/87

lost deposits. In addition, federal deposit insurance was raised to $100,000 from $40,000, providing an added advantage. But the thrifts still found themselves in trouble. They had to pay much more to attract deposits than they were earning on their 30-year home loans, many of which were still yielding the low interest rates of the early 1970s.

The lobbyists: Richard Hohlt and James "Snake" Freeman. The thrift industry decided it needed more legislative relief, and the industry's largest lobby group, the U.S. League of Savings Institutions, went to work, with Freeman and Hohlt leading the way. (No one seems to know for certain why Freeman is called "Snake," though one theory naturally suggests itself and seems to have occurred to almost everyone who knows him.) The league's goal was further deregulation. To recoup the highest interest rates thrifts could now pay, they wanted to expand beyond home loans, into riskier, potentially more profitable, investments: consumer credit cards, commercial real estate developments, etc. The desired legislation would blur the distinction between banks and S&Ls by allowing thrifts to do just about everything banks could do. But it would also preserve the long-standing distinction that entitles S&Ls to tax breaks and other subsidies. Never mind that those subsidies had originally been granted in exchange for the industry's promise to focus on providing home loans, a promise that this legislation would go a long way toward breaking.

Bad with Numbers

The stooges: M. Danny Wall and Fernand J. St Germain. The league focused its efforts on two people in particular: St Germain of Rhode Island, chairman of the House Banking Committee, and Wall, then the chief banking aide to Senator Jake Garn of Utah, the chairman of the Senate Banking Committee. Wall—who, ironically, has a reputation for being bad with numbers—is now chairman of the Federal Home Loan Bank Board, which is charged with regulating the S&L industry. His performance in this role alone might be enough to condemn him to S&L hell, but his contribution to the S&L crisis began back when he was advising Garn. This is the job that earned him the attention of the league's lobbyists.

Hohlt went to work on Garn, or more accurately, on Wall, with whom Hohlt is still a close friend. Hohlt's number became the first one listed on Wall's Senate speed-dial telephone. (As bank board chairman, Wall continues to confer frequently with Hohlt, sometimes several times a day.) While on Garn's staff, Wall earned a reputation for accepting all-expenses-paid trips from the league and other lobby groups. A few years ago a reporter examined the disclosure statements of top congressional staffers and found that Wall led the pack in lobbyist-subsidized junkets, with 30 in a single year.

St Germain turned out to be amenable to subsidy as well. Snake Freeman gave him free use of charge accounts at restaurants around town, and the two men became regular dinner partners. If someone needed to find one of them after business hours, he was told to try the Prime Rib restaurant on K Street. Freeman also provided St Germain with golfing trips and sometimes arranged late-evening entertainment for the congressman. The legislation that the league sought was passed in 1982 as the Garn-St Germain bill.

The revolving-door regulators: Richard Pratt and Thomas Vartanian. Congress was not alone in granting relief to the thrift industry in 1982. Pratt, then the bank board chairman, and Vartanian, the board's chief counsel, initiated new, lenient accounting rules after the league insisted that S&Ls squeezed by interest rates needed time to grow out of their problems. The new rules masked losses and overstated profits, thus preventing government regulators from closing money-losing thrifts whose net worth—an S&L's cushion against loans going sour—was plummeting. Industry losses continued to mount.

In 1983 Pratt stepped down from the bank board to take a job as head of the mortgage-backed securities department at Merrill Lynch. His ties to the bank board didn't hurt the firm's ability to garner government business. Vartanian left to become a partner in the law firm of Fried, Frank, Harris, Shriver & Jacobson, where he brings in millions of dollars a year representing people who want to buy or sell S&Ls that fell into trouble because of the very policies he advanced. His government connections don't hurt, either.

We pause to mention a would-be hero: Edwin J. Gray. Appointed by the White House to replace Pratt was Gray, an S&L executive from California who had been a top fund-raiser for Ronald Reagan. League President William O'Connell thought he had a puppet in Gray. The league had worked hard for Gray's appointment, drawing on Hohlt's longtime friendship with Craig Fuller, chief of staff for Vice President George Bush.

"Deposit insurance . . . had become a license for S&L executives to gamble on fast growth and easy profits using government-guaranteed funds."

As bank board chairman, Gray did at first remain close to the industry. He conferred with O'Connell frequently, and was only too happy to accept thousands of dollars in travel and entertainment expenses from the league and the S&L industry as he crisscrossed the country to make speeches to thrift executives. (It is hard to say exactly how unethical this was, because much of this money came from the 12 Federal Home Loan Banks, weird institutions that have quasi-governmental status but are funded by the S&L industry and run by a board of directors made up almost entirely of S&L executives.)

Deregulation Backfired

As close as Gray was to the industry, he was not blind to the mounting evidence that deregulation had backfired. The new investments S&Ls were making in real estate and other areas were riskier than anything they were used to, and many of them were going bad. Still, the losses weren't overly painful to S&L executives; there was always the government-backed $100,000 deposit insurance to pick up the pieces. The resulting syndrome became known as the moral hazard problem: deposit insurance was no longer only bolstering confidence among savers; it had become a license for S&L executives to gamble on fast growth and easy profits using government-guaranteed funds.

Wild growth at S&Ls was fueled by "brokered deposit" blocks of $100,000 that are wholly covered by federal deposit insurance and pulled by professional money managers in and out of institutions depending on which offers the highest rate. As S&Ls lost money on bad investments, they offered higher and higher rates to attract brokered funds that they then would desperately invest in even riskier ventures. And so on. By the time the curtain was drawn on some Texas S&Ls, more than 90 percent of their loans had gone sour.

By 1984 Gray could see that the S&Ls' problems had shifted fundamentally. The thrifts were no longer just losing money on low-yielding loans they had made in the early 1970s. They were losing money on the high-risk loans—which often turned out to be no-yielding—permitted by the Garn-St Germain act. And thanks to the revised accounting rules, they had little capital cushion to absorb the losses. Gray began to break with league policy by saying publicly that hundreds of ailing S&Ls, far from growing out of their problems, had become more troubled and would soon need a government bailout from the Federal Savings and Loan Insurance Corporation, the bank board fund that insures deposits. He warned that the mounting failures could bankrupt FSLIC and jeopardize the entire S&L industry if not curbed. But that would require more examiners, something the Garn-St Germain act hadn't provided. "The list of horror stories resulting from the misuses of brokered funds by desperate financial institutions is growing as the weeks and months go on," Gray told Congress in 1984. "We are facing a potentially acute shortage of examiners. . . . Simply put, a large number of institutions have taken in more funds than can be safely employed in prudent lending, resulting in growth which is almost

uncontrollable. . . . We . . . are seriously understaffed.

The thrift industry did everything it could to shut Gray up. One S&L executive from California, Charlie Keating, hired several top law firms to leak reports about Gray's acceptance of travel and other gifts from the league. The ensuing publicity embarrassed Gray and undermined his credibility, as intended.

The attack dog: Frank Annunzio. Democratic Representative Annunzio of Illinois, who has been close to the league for years and represents the congressional district in Chicago of O'Connell, longtime president of the league, helped put the strong-arm on Gray. Annunzio's chief banking aide, Curt Prins (known around Capitol Hill for his unflattering remarks about Jews and other ethnic groups), threatened that Gray would not be able to get a job after his bank board term expired if he didn't stop talking about the industry's problems.

The System's Folly

All of this took its toll on Gray. Several Washington reporters have had the experience of receiving a call from him while they're on deadline and simply letting him talk to himself while they worked. It was even possible to set the phone down and come back minutes later to find him still ranting (accurately) about the folly in the S&L system.

Gray's growing reputation as something of a wild-eyed fanatic on the subject of S&Ls, combined with the embarrassing disclosures about his ethical shoddiness, made him a man who was easy to ignore. Neither Congress nor the Reagan administration's Office of Management and Budget used its authority to increase the number of examiners as Gray requested. It is clear in retrospect that following his advice would have saved the nation tens of billions of dollars.

"One of the most important lessons of the S&L mess is that sometimes deregulation calls for stronger federal oversight."

See no evil: Don Regan. Regan, treasury secretary during Reagan's first term and chief of staff during his second, was well situated to perceive the S&L crisis and do something about it. He was also well situated to stifle reform by pretending the problem didn't exist. He took the latter path. Regan (whose tenure as chief of staff includes such other highlights as the Iran-*contra* scandal) became infuriated with Gray's requests to beef up enforcement and developed an intense dislike for him. He argued that increasing the examination staff would be tantamount to reregulating the industry—anathema to free-market-minded Reaganites. Today it is clear that Regan confused regulation with supervision; Gray wasn't asking for more regulation, just more policing to enforce the existing regulations. One of the most important lessons of the S&L mess is that sometimes deregulation calls for stronger federal oversight.

Spokesman for the bag men: Larry Taggart. In addition to his devotion to deregulation, Regan had another reason to resist attempts to crack down on industry abuses—the loss of GOP campaign contributions from S&L executives. Taggart, a former S&L commissioner of California, wrote in a letter to Regan dated August 4, 1986, that "these actions . . . by [Gray] are likely to have a very adverse impact on the ability of our [Republican] Party to raise needed campaign funds in the upcoming elections. Many who have been very supportive of the Administration are involved with savings and loans associations which are either being closed by the [bank board] or threatened with closure."

"The cleanup costs would soon become so large the industry couldn't afford it, and taxpayers would get the bill instead."

Wild Bill O'Connell. Many lobbyists, to help themselves sleep at night, live by a simple ethical stricture: be selective in your citation of facts, even stretch the truth if necessary, but never lie. That was not League President O'Connell's way. Late in 1988, when he retired as president, O'Connell was still insisting publicly that the bank board's deposit insurance fund had adequate resources to close or sell hundreds of ailing S&Ls, even though the General Accounting Office and private analysts had for years been declaring the fund hopelessly insolvent. In fact, privately O'Connell had been warning S&L executives about the crisis facing the fund. According to Gray, former league officials, and former members of the Reagan Administration, the purpose of this deception was simple: if the league could delay the government's attempt to tackle the problem, the cleanup costs would soon become large the industry couldn't afford it, and taxpayers would get the bill instead. Delay increased the cost of the bailout by more than $1 billion a month.

Would-be heroes two and three: James Baker and George Gould. Despite Regan's efforts to ignore the problem, some Reagan officials understood its seriousness. In early 1986 Treasury Secretary James Baker proposed a $15 billion bailout plan to be funded by the S&L industry. If adopted, it would have gone a long way toward a solution. But the U.S. League, still unwilling to let the scope of the industry's problem become public, lobbied to reduce Baker's bailout package to $5 billion, insisting that was all that was needed. Lobbyist Hohlt's willingness to understate the size of the problem before Congress

and the public became so odious to some in the Reagan administration that for over a year he was banned from entering the office of Undersecretary of the Treasury George Gould, who spearheaded the White House bailout plan.

Stalling the Bailout

Jim "money talks" Wright. Wright joined the U.S. League in trying to stall the bailout package. In Texas, S&Ls were big contributors to the Democratic Party, and had long had Wright's ear. Lately a couple of financially troubled Texas thrifts had complained to him about the oppressive scrutiny of bank board examiners. He decided to use the threat of sitting on the bailout package as leverage to get Gray's policemen to back off. Wright delayed action on the bailout until the fall of 1987, when he OK'd compromise legislation providing $10.8 billion in new funding for the bankrupt S&L insurance fund. It was too little too late.

In January 1989 Bush announced that massive funds will be needed to clean up the industry. Amazingly, the league is contending that the government and not the industry should bear the blame for and full cost of the disaster. It is worth noting, as Gray did during congressional hearings, that "when it came to thrift matters in the Congress, the U.S. League and many of its affiliates were the de facto government. The league's consuming strategy was to buy time and buy time and buy time, and if enough time was bought, if the disaster was permitted to get big enough, so that only the taxpayers could pay the bill, its members would have been well-served." Gray added, "The folks at the league told me this was the strategy, not once, but on a number of occasions."

Danny Wall rides again. In July 1987 Gray's term expired. Reluctantly, and only at the urging of Garn and the U.S. League, President Reagan appointed Wall to take his place. Wall took advantage of the opportunity to do a series of embarrassing things. First he extolled the success of the disastrous 1982 Garn-St Germain act. Then, though the Federal Savings and Loan Insurance Corporation was clearly bankrupt, Wall committed it to pay $6000 to the Jake Garn Institute, a think tank being set up (by former bank board chairman Richard Pratt and others) at the senator's alma mater, the University of Utah. When asked about the donation, Wall replied, "So?"

Wall's tenure as chairman is strewn with denials of how big the S&L problem really is. In 1987 he said it would take $16 billion to clean up the industry and that no tax money would be needed. A few months later he raised the estimate to $32 billion, then a few months later to $50 billion. The Treasury Department was quietly citing estimates twice that. Officials at the Federal Deposit Insurance

Corporation (FDIC), which insures deposits at commercial banks, began referring to Wall as M. Danny Isuzu.

George Bush and his predecessor. Why would Danny Wall downplay the crisis to the extent of undermining his own credibility? Here's a hint: he quit doing it shortly after the presidential election; suddenly, with George Bush's victory secure, Wall's S&L cleanup estimates miraculously matched the Treasury's much more alarming figures. Wall wasn't alone in keeping things quiet until after November 1988. In between the agreement on the hugely inadequate FSLIC bailout of August '87 and George Bush's election in November '88, the administration avoided prominent discussion of the S&L problem.

Maybe you could argue that Ronald Reagan isn't to blame, because he didn't deeply understand the issue (the all-purpose Reagan alibi), but the same certainly can't be said about Bush. Bush had several years earlier chaired the administration's task force on financial deregulation, which closely examined the problems of thrifts and banks. And the author of the committee's report, Richard Breeden—one of the most astute analysts of the S&L mess around—has for some time been in Bush's circle. In fact, Bush chose him to fashion a solution to the problem, even as Bush was saying nothing publicly about it and was, moreover, blithely assuring us that the budget could be kept under control without a tax hike. During Bush's virtual moratorium on discussion of the S&L crisis—from August 1987 until January 1989—the cost of cleaning the mess up grew by at least $20 billion, maybe $30 billion. But that's nothing compared with Reagan, who went eight years without ever mentioning the problem publicly.

Farseeing Reform

The bailout plan Bush unveiled February 1989 includes a farseeing reform package that, if adopted, would move toward the eventual elimination of the distinction between thrifts and banks. At the same time, it would create the new position of S&L czar within the Treasury Department, and the Bush administration has promised Wall that if Congress agrees to the plan, he'll get the job. Most people in the FDIC (which under the plan would regulate thrifts as well as banks) aren't keen on that idea—and, neither, for that matter, are many people in the Bush administration. They're offering Wall the new job for one reason only: they need Jake Garn's support on the bailout.

The PACmen: Annunzio, Don Riegle, Alan Cranston. The U.S. League, rightly afraid that the Bush plan will weaken its control over S&L regulators (that's the whole idea), asked the White House to consider providing the bailout money now and leaving any restructuring for later. The administration said no. So the lobby group has launched a campaign against Bush's plan, and has turned for support to its many allies on the Democratic side of the House and Senate. In particular, it is happy to count in its corner such old friends as Senator Riegle of Michigan, Representative Annunzio, and Senator Cranston of California—all of whom, along with such other notables as Jim Wright, belie the simplistic idea that the S&L fiasco was nothing more than a regulatory failure by a Republican administration.

"The S&L industry . . . is no longer succeeding in its original role as a conduit for government subsidies to homebuyers."

What else do these three men have in common? Various connections to the thrifts, among them that all three have benefitted from the industry's ample political action committees. Another unifying theme: strange ideas about the nature of the S&L problem. Annunzio wants to preserve the S&L industry virtually without change, regardless of the fact that it is no longer succeeding in its original role as a conduit for government subsidies to homebuyers. Today the percentage of young American adults who can afford a first home is lower than it's been in a decade, and S&Ls make only 40 percent of all home loans, compared with 58 percent just a decade ago.

Luckily for taxpayers, St Germain is no longer around to throw in his two cents. The Justice Department's investigation of thousands of dollars in dining and other entertainment expenses—which the representative accepted from Freeman and other league officials but did not report, as the law requires—so tainted him that he lost his bid for re-election last fall.

But Danny Wall, that hardy perennial, is still around and promises to be in the thick of things for years, if not decades, to come. Wall was asked not long ago who was responsible for allowing the crisis to grow for so long. "The point isn't whose responsibility it is," Wall said. "That's all history."

Kathleen Day is a Washington Post *staff writer.*

"America's failed savings and loans have become the country's biggest, most scandalous financial mess."

Government Aid to the Savings and Loan Industry: An Overview

Barbara Rudolph

"You know, George, I feel that in a small way we're doing something important, satisfying a fundamental urge. It's deep in the race for a man to want his own roof and walls and fireplace. And we're helping him get these things . . ."
—Peter Bailey to his son George in *It's a Wonderful Life*

In the 1946 film, George Bailey took that advice to heart and, despite the requisite dramatic difficulties, made his family's building and loan association a pillar of the community. But in real life, the outcome has been much different. America's failed savings and loans have become the country's biggest, most scandalous financial mess. Devastated by a legacy of bad management, rampant fraud and inept Government supervision, more than 500 of the 3,150 federally insured thrifts had fallen into insolvency as of the beginning of 1988. Because the U.S. failed to own up to the problem and launch a major rescue soon enough, the cost has now grown higher than almost anyone had imagined. Says Michigan Democrat Donald Riegle, chairman of the Senate Banking Committee: "We've never faced a problem of this scale. The answers aren't going to be happy ones."

In February 1989 President Bush came forward with a long-awaited bailout plan in which he sought to spread around the unhappiness in an evenhanded way. Said Bush: "Nothing is without pain when you come to solve a problem of this magnitude." His program will require taxpayers and S&Ls to share the burden of a rescue that will cost an estimated $126 billion during the next decade. The taxpayer portion would amount to about $60 billion, which would be contained in the federal budget over the next ten years. The Government would borrow $50

billion by issuing 30-year bonds to be repaid through revenues collected from S&Ls. Including the interest expense, half of which will be borne by taxpayers, the total package could cost $200 billion or more over the course of three decades.

The Government is obliged to spend $40 billion to cover bailout cases to which federal regulators are already committed, including 205 savings and loans that the Government closed or sold in 1988. The $50 billion bond issue would be spent to liquidate or auction off the remaining 300 or more insolvent savings and loans. Those failing thrifts will be isolated from the rest of the industry by bringing them under a new agency called the Resolution Trust Corp., which will oversee their cleanup.

Besides rounding up all that cash, Bush proposes to reform the system that supervises the thrift industry and insures its deposits. The main regulatory agency, the Federal Home Loan Bank Board, which has been accused of being too chummy with thrift-industry leaders, will be replaced by one chairman who will answer to the Treasury Secretary. The exhausted Federal Savings and Loan Insurance Corp. [FSLIC], which guarantees deposits, will be overseen by its healthier and better-staffed counterpart for the banking industry, the Federal Deposit Insurance Corp. [FDIC]. Banks and thrifts have traditionally had separate regulators and roles: S&Ls specialized in taking long-term savings deposits and issuing residential mortgages, while banks typically held shorter-term accounts and concentrated on making commercial loans. . . .

For the most part, his proposal found bipartisan support. Said Iowa Republican Jim Leach, a member of the House Banking Committee: "In his first inning, Bush has stepped up and hit a home run." Another member of the committee, New York Democrat Charles Schumer, said that Bush deserves "a heck of a lot of credit for bellying up to the bar and putting a real plan on the table." . . .

Barbara Rudolph, "Finally, the Bill Has Come Due," *Time*, February 20, 1989. Copyright 1989 Time Inc. Reprinted by permission.

One widespread early complaint was that Administration officials, notably Budget Director Richard Darman, were using sleight of hand to downplay the bailout's true cost. Darman originally seemed to say that the cost to taxpayers would total about $40 billion in the first decade, but that number in fact described only how much the plan would aggravate budget deficits. The actual spending from general revenues would be closer to $60 billion. But purely from an accounting standpoint, its impact will be offset by $20 billion in increased insurance-premium fees to be collected from the banking industry—even though the funds will be earmarked for future banking bailouts rather than for cleaning up the thrifts.

Moreover, financial consultants pointed out that the Administration was projecting the cost of the rescue based on the rosy scenario of a robust economy, declining interest rates and fast-growing thrift deposits. Over the next decade, taxpayers may have to shoulder rescue costs that are tens of billions more dollars than now expected. Yet even those who recognized the Bush plan's shortcomings praised it as the best and boldest solution so far.

A primary objective of such a sweeping rescue was to restore the confidence of thrift depositors, some of whom have withdrawn their savings in fear of the system's insolvency. In fact, the Administration secretly feared a long-shot possibility that the drama of its bailout might spark a run on S&L deposits. To prepare for that dire prospect, senior White House officials and Federal Reserve Board Chairman Alan Greenspan met in the Roosevelt Room of the White House the night before Bush's plan was made public. Greenspan agreed that the Fed would stand ready to pump billions of dollars in emergency loans into threatened thrifts.

In the end, depositors stayed calm, even though some chafed at the idea of the cost of the bailout. "Honestly, it's the stupidest thing I've heard," said Leroy Scrues, a Detroit retiree. "Why should the public be paying for these rich people's mistakes?" Yet legislators and savers were relieved that Bush repudiated a proposal that his Administration had floated earlier: to levy a fee—25¢ for each $100 of deposits—on all insured accounts. That ploy was widely seen as a tax in everything but name. The short-lived proposal was so distasteful that it made Bush's new plan seem all the more palatable. Said Fred Dorey, a Los Angeles medical statistician: "We were going to pay for it one way or another. At least the banks have to pay some too. It's a fair deal."

The healthy portion of the thrift industry will pay its share through an increase in its insurance premiums. The rate would rise from the current $2.08 per $1,000 of deposits to $2.30 from 1991 until 1994, after which it would decline to $1.80. The rate for banks would increase too, from 83¢ per $1,000 to $1.20 in 1990 and $1.50 thereafter. Even though

both industries' insurance funds would be administered by the FDIC, their proceeds will be kept separate.

One reason for raising the banking industry's fees as part of the rescue package is to ensure that they do not obtain too much of a competitive advantage over thrifts in terms of their costs of doing business. Another reason is simply to bolster the banking industry's reserve fund so that it does not run into the same problems encountered by the FSLIC. In the end, at least some of the increased costs will probably be passed along to consumers, since thrift profits are already squeezed. Said Texas Democrat Henry Gonzalez, chairman of the House Banking Committee: "The little consumer will pay in the form of higher fees on checking accounts, new fees for automatic tellers and a myriad of other charges."

The thrift industry seemed to meet the proposal with grudging acceptance but a fair amount of grumbling. Healthy S&Ls object philosophically to paying excessive cleanup costs for their fraudulent and incompetent brethren. Says Adam Jahns, chairman of Chicago's Craigin Federal Savings & Loan: "I don't think we should have to pay for serious crimes committed by others." Another complaint by S&Ls is that by combining thrift and banking supervision, the Bush plan may blur the distinction between the two and eventually remove any competitive advantage the thrifts still have, principally the ability to borrow long-term funds from federal Home Loan banks. Commercial banks are restricted to taking shorter-term loans from Federal Reserve banks. Besides paying higher premiums under the Bush plan, S&L owners would be required to follow stricter accounting rules and to boost their reserve capital from 3% of assets to 6%.

> "Healthy S&Ls object philosophically to paying excessive cleanup costs for their fraudulent and incompetent brethren."

Bankers were miffed too about being tied up with the S&Ls. The symbolic point of contention was the trusted FDIC decal that banks display prominently on their premises and in their advertising. The Administration at first told thrift owners that they would be able to display the symbol under the new plan. To many depositors, the seal represents greater safety and security than the thrift industry's own logo. Bankers therefore vociferously oppose sharing the FDIC seal, maintaining that it would be effectively tarnished if given to the thrifts and would lead to the complete merging of the two insurance funds. By week's end, the Administration had backed away from its promise of the seal to the S&L industry.

The FDIC wasted no time in wielding its new authority over the thrifts. Within a day after the Bush announcement, the Government agency took charge of four insolvent S&Ls and three days later assumed control of six more. . . . The FDIC also decided to freeze temporarily all negotiations for the sale of ailing thrifts. In 1988 the FSLIC completed a flurry of deals—34 in December alone—in an effort to offer investors tax breaks that expired on Dec. 31. Because of the rich payoffs guaranteed to investors in those deals, they were highly controversial. Said L. William Seidman, chairman of the FDIC: "Before we go forward, we are going to evaluate, along with the FSLIC, where we stand."

Seidman said talks with investors will resume after the FDIC takes control of the remaining insolvent S&Ls. But since the FDIC said it would then allow only deals that were supported by the cash of the FSLIC—a fund that is currently bankrupt—more Government-assisted sales would seem unlikely. The FDIC might also try to renegotiate some of 1988's sweet deals.

When the huge cost of the cleanup hit home, so did a strong sentiment in favor of pursuing the fraudulent thrift owners who made off with the loot. Regulators have estimated that at least one in every four S&L failures has been the result of fraud. In fact, the Bush rescue plan proposes to give the Justice Department an additional $50 million a year for probing S&L fraud, a sum that would pay for 200 new investigators and 100 more prosecutors.

Even so, in testimony before the Senate Banking Committee, Attorney General Richard Thornburgh said most of the lost money is long gone. "In many cases, the assets have been dissipated through laundering schemes or taken out of the country, and are beyond the reach of federal authorities," he said. "We'd be fooling ourselves to think that any substantial portion of these assets is going to be recovered." Besides the money that was simply stolen, billions of dollars were lost on high-risk investments and frittered away by paying excessively high interest rates to attract depositors.

How did the S&Ls arrive at such a sorry state? Traditionally, running a thrift was a relatively tranquil business. S&L managers used to follow what was known as the 3-6-3 rule: pay depositors 3%, lend money at 6% and tee up at the golf course by 3 p.m. When interest rates remained stable, the strategy worked well. But by the late 1970s, thrifts began steadily losing depositors to the new money-market funds, which were not covered by deposit insurance and paid higher interest rates.

Thrift executives pressured Congress to let them fight back. In 1980 Congress lifted restrictions on interest rates that S&Ls could pay. But regulators waited a year before freeing the other side of the balance sheet by allowing S&Ls to grant adjustable-rate mortgages. The delay left the thrifts in a bind,

because interest rates had rocketed from 13% at the end of 1979 to more than 20% a year later. Thrifts were collecting interest rates of around 8% or less on their 30-year mortgages, while paying double-digit interest to new depositors. During 1981 some 85% of all S&Ls were losing money.

Interest rates eventually eased, but other problems arose. Congress passed a sweeping deregulatory law in 1982 that permitted S&Ls to make loans for a raft of new businesses. At the same time, some states allowed their locally chartered thrifts to run wild. Suddenly no venture was too farfetched: ethanol plants, wind farms, Las Vegas casinos and commuter airlines. S&L managers who were accustomed to making simple residential mortgages were ill prepared to evaluate the new kinds of credit risks. The great mistake in deregulation was not so much the easing of rules but the failure of the federal and state governments to boost supervision at the same time.

"A perverse trait among shaky S&Ls has been their tendency to get further and further into what one bank regulator . . . calls 'deep yogurt.'"

A perverse trait among shaky S&Ls has been their tendency to get further and further into what one bank regulator euphemistically calls "deep yogurt," in part because they must offer higher interest rates than their competitors to keep attracting savings. Big-time depositors flock to these S&Ls, knowing that they cannot lose because the Government will guarantee deposits up to $100,000. In that sense, Congress contributed to the FSLIC's liability in 1980, when it raised the coverage limit from $40,000.

Troubled S&Ls are heavily concentrated in Texas and California, where state thrift regulations were loose and local economies had booms and busts. Many Texas thrift owners who pumped money into energy ventures when oil sold for $29 per bbl. in 1983 saw their collateral collapse in value when prices plummeted below $10 in 1986. In California some thrifts invested in real estate markets that became glutted, including Los Angeles office towers and Beverly Hills condominiums.

The overall losses would have been vastly smaller if Government regulators had seized control of insolvent S&Ls years ago. In 1983 the cost of the bailouts was estimated at only $10 billion. But the FSLIC never had enough cash simply to close down the thrifts and pay off the depositors. The Bank Board lobbied Congress for more money, but the politically powerful thrift industry consistently opposed such requests, along with almost any proposal to rein in the S&Ls.

Edwin Gray, chairman of the Bank Board from 1983 to 1987, bitterly accuses congressional leaders of bowing to industry pressure. He claims that S&L lobbyists tried to coerce him by warning that his future career in the business would be ruined if he opposed them. . . .

Instead of liquidating insolvent S&Ls, regulators decided it would be cheaper and more expedient to sell them to private investors or merge them with healthy thrifts. Bank Board Chairman M. Danny Wall sharply stepped up the tempo of such sales in 1988, selling or liquidating more than 200 thrifts at an estimated cost to the Government of $39 billion in tax breaks and other incentives extended to the buyers. Critics contend that the regulators were taken for a ride. Fumed Iowa's Leach: "The dealmakers are laughing all the way to the piggy bank." But Wall staunchly defends his deals as the lesser of evils. "I much prefer to be damned for having done something than to be damned for doing nothing," he says. In fact, the cleanup is showing some results. The thrift industry's 1988 third-quarter loss of $1.6 billion was down from $3.9 billion in each of the previous two quarters.

"The President's rescue plan prompts many banking experts to wonder whether the U.S. needs a separate S&L industry anymore."

Will thrifts ever thrive again? By blurring the distinction between banks and thrifts, the President's rescue plan prompts many banking experts to wonder whether the U.S. needs a separate S&L industry anymore. Thrifts hold about one-third of all U.S. mortgages, down from nearly 60% some 20 years ago. Says Laurence Fink, a partner in the Blackstone Group, an investment firm that is acquiring several S&Ls: "The average homeowner can get a mortgage without stepping inside an S&L. Maybe the thrifts have outlived their usefulness."

The thrift industry that survives the coming decade will probably look very different from what it is today. Says Jonathan Gray, who follows the industry for the Sanford C. Bernstein investment firm: "If there's one word to describe the industry's future, it's turmoil." Gray envisions a severe industry shake-out. In just a decade, he points out, the number of U.S. thrifts has already fallen from 4,200 to less than 3,000. By the late 1990s, he predicts, there will be just 1,000 left.

The S&L business will never be as peaceful as it once was. Surviving thrifts will have to compete with powerful rivals and satisfy a far more sophisticated customer than they did in the past. But if the industry shakes off its con artists and recaptures its basic prudence, those thrifts that remain might still do George Bailey proud.

Barbara Rudolph is a staff writer for Time *magazine in New York City.*

The Government Should Save the Savings and Loan Industry

Nicholas F. Brady

From the day when I was sworn in as Secretary of the Treasury, a top priority has been to achieve a sound, responsible response to the savings and loan crisis. President Bush is correct: No simple or painless solution to this problem exists. Only eighteen days after he was inaugurated, however, he announced the Administration's plan. In doing so, President Bush reaffirmed our commitment to fix it now, fix it right, and fix it once and for all.

Two watch words guided us as we prepared a plan to solve this problem—NEVER AGAIN.

• *Never again* should a federal insurance fund that protects depositors become insolvent.

• *Never again* should insolvent federally-insured depository institutions remain open and operate without sufficient private risk capital.

• *Never again* should risky activities permitted by individual states put the federal deposit insurance fund in jeopardy.

• *Never again* should fraud committed against financial institutions or depositors be punished as if it were a victimless white-collar crime.

• *Never again* should the nation's savings and loan system, which is important to our commitment to available, affordable housing, be put in jeopardy.

The Administration plan meets these standards. It serves as a blueprint for comprehensive reform and sound financing. It assures the emergence of a healthy and strong S&L industry and for this reason is pro-industry—both for S&Ls and for the housing industry they serve. Moreover, it has the strong support of the federal regulators—the Federal Reserve Board (Federal Reserve), the Federal Deposit Insurance Corporation (FDIC), the Federal Home Loan Bank Board (Bank Board), and the Comptroller of the Currency (OCC). . . .

Our objectives are to minimize operating losses, restrict unwarranted or unsound growth, eliminate speculative activities and destructive competition in deposit rates, and to get rid of waste, fraud, and insider abuse wherever it exists. . . .

Fast action by all parties—the Administration, the regulators, and the Congress—will help reduce the industry's cost of funds by getting the insolvent institutions resolved, out of the marketplace, and out of the business of needlessly bidding up interest rates.

Given the magnitude of the problems we face, expedited and stabilizing action provides an orderly transition to the new regulatory structure we propose. We now need legislative action by the Congress to put the reform and financing plan into place to finish the job. . . .

Safe and Sound

Cooperative and expedited action by the Congress and the Executive branch will help to reassure the millions of American savers, who rely on deposit insurance protection, that we indeed have a safe and sound financial system that will continue to meet their saving and borrowing needs in the future. . . .

To ensure that the tremendous losses in the industry never happen again and to minimize the total cost of resolving the problem, the Administration plan makes structural reforms a prerequisite for the use of any taxpayer funds and provides for the necessary funding to solve the problem *now*. The following Administration objectives guided the development of our plan:

• Reform—a prerequisite to additional funding;

• A flexible financing plan of sufficient capacity to repair the damage;

Nicholas F. Brady, from testimony before the House committee on banking, finance, and urban affairs, *Treasury News*, February 23, 1989.

- Institutional arrangements that lessen the disruption in the industry and avoid creating new government bureaucracies;

- Utilizing a fair level of S&L industry sources of funds before using taxpayer funds;

- Precise and trackable accounting for all public and private funds employed in resolving the S&L problem;

- Structural reforms that are sound, but practical enough to accommodate the market-driven changes that develop in any competitive industry;

- Funding for an adequate, on-going, self-financed savings association insurance fund, so that Treasury funds will not be needed again to bolster the deposit insurance funds;

- Protecting American taxpayers by assuring full financial and regulatory accountability through Treasury oversight; and

- Finally, sufficient private capital and industry-financed insurance funds standing between financial institution failures and the taxpayers. . . .

Some observers have already expressed reservations about Treasury oversight of the primary thrift supervisor in a manner that parallels our authority over national banks. We do not intend to micro-manage the revitalized Federal Home Loan Bank System. That concern led to our designating a chairman who would serve and function as a chief executive officer.

Adequate Oversight

It is critical, however, that we exercise the proper degree of oversight. The reason is clear: Treasury funds are being used for the first time as part of the clean-up operation. . . .

We are experiencing the results today of an industry that collectively has not been adequately capitalized. We have learned a valuable lesson: Deposit insurance simply will not work without sufficient private capital at risk and up front.

The Administration plan will increase safety and soundness standards for savings and loan institutions by requiring these institutions to meet standards equivalent to commercial bank capital and regulatory standards within a two-year period. This is consistent with the on-going efforts of all the federal financial regulators, including the current Bank Board, to implement risk-based capital to ensure that sufficient private capital is at risk ahead of the deposit insurance fund. Again, private capital is the best assurance that the federal insurance of deposits will not be exposed to undue risk and imprudent investment behavior. . . .

Some stockholders may suffer dilution of their holdings, but appropriately we are achieving a safer and stronger system where private capital stands ahead of the government's insurance of deposits,

giving taxpayers enhanced protection. At the same time, we expect a lower cost of funds for the solvent portion of the industry once unfair competition from insolvent institutions is removed. . . .

There is a fundamental requirement that the federal deposit insurance funds are put on a sound financial basis. This can be accomplished by reestablishing the basic principle of industry-financed deposit insurance funds standing between any future industry problems and the taxpayer.

"The Administration plan will increase safety and soundness standards for savings and loan institutions."

The cost of the S&L solution underscores the importance of requiring all federal deposit funds to be adequately capitalized. Consistent with this mandate is the creation of a sound savings association insurance fund, not just after-the-fact financing for insolvent S&Ls. It is equally important that we shore up the commercial bank insurance fund. The FDIC insurance fund's reserve-to-insured deposit ratio has fallen to an estimated all-time low of 0.83 percent from its historical average of 1.40 percent.

We propose increasing commercial bank premiums to bring the FDIC fund back in line with its historical reserve-to-deposit ratio to protect depositors and taxpayers. Specifically, we propose a gradual rise in the deposit insurance premiums paid by commercial banks from $.08 per $100 in deposits to $.15 per $100 in deposits by 1991. Premiums would be rebated when the bank insurance fund is in excess of a 1.25 percent reserve-to-deposit ratio.

It is important to point out that this is the first statutory increase in the FDIC's deposit insurance premium since 1935. During the intervening years, the amount of deposits insured per depositor in any one institution has increased from $2,500 in 1933 to the current level of $100,000. . . .

Let me describe in some detail the Administration plan for restoring the S&L industry to financial health. It has three components. The first $50 billion is to resolve currently insolvent institutions and any other marginally solvent institutions which may become insolvent over the next several years. Secondly, the plan ensures adequate servicing of the $40 billion in past FSLIC [Federal Savings and Loan Insurance Corporation] obligations. And third, and perhaps most important, the plan provides $33 billion in financial resources necessary to put S&L deposit insurance on a sound financial basis for the future.

At the heart of our plan is the creation of a Resolution Trust Corporation (RTC), for which the FDIC will be the primary manager directed to resolve all S&Ls which are now GAAP [generally accepted accounting principles] insolvent or become so over the next three years. The creation of this new corporation will serve several practical business purposes: it will allow the isolation and containment of all insolvent S&Ls during the three-year resolution process and will facilitate a full and precise accounting of all the funds that are used. The RTC will seek to complete the resolution or other disposition of all insolvent institutions and their assets over a period of five years. An Oversight Board consisting of the Secretary of the Treasury, the Chairman of the Federal Reserve Board of Governors, and the Attorney General will monitor all RTC activities to ensure the most effective use of both private and public financial resources.

To accomplish its task, the RTC will have available $50 billion in new funding, which is provided by the Administration plan. The plan also provides funds to pay for the $40 billion that already has been committed in past FSLIC resolutions. Finally, the plan will provide additional funds for handling insolvencies in the post-RTC period from 1992 to 1999, as well as to help build an insurance fund for the healthy S&Ls—the Savings Association Insurance Fund (SAIF)—which will be operating during this period. . . .

Give a Fair Share

The S&L industry will be a major beneficiary of restoring its own financial health. From the outset, the Administration has stated that the S&L industry must therefore contribute its fair share—before the Federal government makes good on its pledge to protect insured depositors. As you can see, the plan requires a combination of private industry and public sources throughout. We believe that the share demanded of the industry is indeed fair, but not so great as to jeopardize the viability of the healthy S&L industry which will emerge from the RTC resolution process. And it will indeed be a healthy industry that emerges—one with an attractive and viable charter, with a clean insurance fund, and one prepared to provide its traditional support for home financing. . . .

"It will indeed be a healthy industry that emerges."

How much will it cost assuming all of this caseload of 500 institutions has to be resolved? That, of course, depends on a number of factors—future interest rates, real estate prices and the speed with which the FDIC can get to work on the job. Under likely scenarios, we estimate the size of the immediate problem at well under the $50 billion available to the RTC to handle it. To get our estimate, we start with the $18 billion of negative

tangible net worth. To that cost we add some fraction of the assets which will be lost in the process of liquidation or merger. Our present estimate of the total cost is about $40 billion. Even under less likely scenarios which would make the problem worse, it is within the $50 billion available to the RTC. . . .

In conclusion, the President's comprehensive solution to the savings and loan crisis—if enacted by Congress in a timely manner—will provide a sound, long-term answer to the savings and loan problem. We already have made a head start. The time to act is now.

Nicholas F. Brady is the secretary of the Department of the Treasury.

"The 'Never Again' reforms offered by Treasury Secretary Nicholas Brady are status quo bandaids on a bankrupt structure of federal deposit insurance."

viewpoint 25

The Government Should Not Save the Savings and Loan Industry

Melanie Tammen and Tom Miller

Editor's note: The following viewpoint is in two parts. Part I is by Melanie Tammen and Tom Miller. Part II is by Melanie Tammen.

I

The Bush Administration is up to the same old shell game of its predecessors. Its S&L [Savings and Loan] bailout plan talks glibly of vast sums that will be paid by a bankrupt S&L industry and a banking industry already non-competitive in a world economy. By sleight of hand and tough talk about "Never Again" and "Protect the Taxpayer," the Administration has created out of whole cloth billions of dollars that will supposedly solve the problem.

The latest Bush Administration projection for the total cost of the S&L bailout is $126 billion over the next ten years. While about $60 billion of this is the U.S. taxpayer tab, accounting gimmickry (recording on budget the increased premiums from U.S. banks) will make it look like only $40 billion. The bankrupt U.S. thrift industry, then, will miraculously pay the remainder.

Numbers Do Not Add Up

When you blow away the smoke, however, the numbers don't add up. Watch closely now—and guess which shell houses the coveted future premium stream of the nation's beleaguered thrift industry, the key financial ingredient of the Bush Plan. Shell number one is the $38 billion in commitments made by the FSLIC [Federal Savings and Loan Insurance Corporation] in 1988's infamous mega thrift rescues. Shell number two is the principal payment on the $50 billion in new bonds to be floated under the Bush plan. Shell number

three is the interest requirement on these bonds, to be paid mainly by the taxpayer but also in part by the thrifts. And if you aren't thoroughly confounded, shell number four is an "insurance fund for healthy S&Ls" that the Treasury Department's February 6, 1989 release explains will be "created" with future FSLIC premiums. Under the Bush Plan, this income stream is catering four parties scheduled for the same hour—at opposite ends of town.

The promise of reform turns out to be another empty shell. The quid pro quo is more quid than quo. The "Never Again" reforms offered by Treasury Secretary Nicholas Brady are status quo bandaids on a bankrupt structure of federal deposit insurance.

First, the finances. The Administration proposes to float $50 billion in new bonds, with the thrifts to handle the principal. How is this possible? A "modest" $5-6 billion investment in zero-coupon Treasury bonds will yield the needed $50 billion upon their maturity some thirty years from now. Under the plan, this entire investment is to come from the thrift industry, specifically, "the retained earnings of the Federal Home Loan Banks, funds from the disposal of assets received from insolvent S&Ls, and deposit insurance premiums from the thrifts."

But the "retained earnings" total only $2.2 billion. And FSLIC premiums? Comptroller General Charles Bowsher informed the Senate Banking Committee that the sweetheart deals orchestrated by the Bank Board in 1988 will require all of FSLIC's premium stream for the next ten years, plus a further $26 billion. So what about the assets acquired through liquidations and mergers? The FSLIC and its asset liquidation arm have already proven particularly inept at disposing of them. In any event, the tap for liquidating these resources will still be clogged by disputes over getting "fair" prices for them and complaints that such sales will drive down prices of competing private assets.

Melanie Tammen and Tom Miller, "There's Nothing Under S & L Shells," *Los Angeles Times*, February 13, 1989. Melanie Tammen, "A Taxpayer Bailout," *CEI Update*, January 1989. Reprinted with permission.

And all of this presumes the best of all possible worlds: economic assumptions of low inflation, declining interest rates, no new claims against federal deposit insurance funds, and naive investors not demanding risk premiums on bonds that lack full faith and credit.

Then there's the unbudgeted costs of the increased failures to be brought on by the Administration's proposal to squeeze thrifts further by requiring them to double their capital reserves within two years. This will put over the brink many of the 400 thrifts just scraping by now. Moreover, taking the retained earnings of the regional Home Loan Banks is no free lunch. This will likely degrade their credit rating, in turn driving up member thrifts' borrowing costs when issuing future obligations.

And from whence will all this new capital come anyway? Thrifts have three options: retaining some earnings (what earnings?), issuing new equity, or issuing new subordinated debt. But who in their right mind is going to put capital into thrift equities or bonds (except those associated with the prize catch ''Southwest Plan'' mergers)?

Vague Reforms

Finally, we have the other rather vague reforms of a new, consolidated insurance agency for thrifts and banks and ''stricter standards for granting insurance.'' But how strict can a system be that charges one uniform price to all recipients for insurance and, upon insolvency, bails out various uninsured parties—namely uninsured depositors and general creditors. In other words, U.S. taxpayers' liabilities as deposit insurers not only total $2.7 trillion (the total of deposits up to $100,000 in banks, thrifts and credit unions), but current regulatory practices leave taxpayers hostage to the guarantee of $4 trillion in deposits—the total depository base of federally-insured institutions.

If this costly burden of de facto 100 percent deposit insurance is not bad enough, depository institutions—the good and bad alike—will continue to expand taxpayers' liabilities simply by growing. Mismanaged institutions will continue to write hot checks on the taxpayers' account. U.S. taxpayers' provision of these bottomless guarantees has proven to be not the costless and riskless entitlement for depositors that we had considered it. Yesterday's contingent liabilities have become today's real liabilities—on a $100 billion scale—and it's all perfectly legal.

While cleaning up the mess, the Bush Administration has offered nothing to defuse the ''moral hazard'' of federal insurance and protect taxpayers from future bailouts. As banks and thrifts grow, so do taxpayers' liabilities. What does the Administration propose to do about this? Not a damn thing.

Yet the solution to this unlimited line of credit on the taxpayer is simple: cap the federal trough. Nearly $3 trillion is subsidy enough for the U.S. financial services industry. The Bush Administration can cap taxpayer liabilities and allocate that sum to insured institutions, based on their present deposit base. This federal insurance would be made tradeable; and institutions desiring to grow would have to either purchase federal insurance in the market, or phase in private deposit insurance.

As private insurance enters at the margin, market signals would be introduced, and with them a transparent process that would make it more difficult for regulators to forbear in utilizing their regulatory tools.

''The Bush Plan reforms are simply more hair of the dog that bit us.''

So Washington politicians are breathing a sigh of relief. They don't have to crack the tough nut— deposit insurance reform—and face up to their complicity in politically-manipulated regulation that inevitably played fast and loose with underfinanced taxpayer guarantees.

The Bush Plan reforms are simply more hair of the dog that bit us. They leave us no comfort but to hope that regulators will get it right next time. But they have had numerous regulatory guns all along that they never took out of their holsters. Dressing these up in new clothes with proclamations of ''Never Again'' is thin gruel for a $100 billion problem.

II

You can count on it. Three hundred and forty-seven dollars for every American man, woman and child, according to the U.S. General Accounting Office. Its $127 billion estimate of the cost to bury hundreds of bankrupt U.S. thrifts includes $85 billion from taxpayers—several times the cost of the bailouts of Lockheed, New York City, Chrysler and Continental Illinois combined. And taxpayers are on the hook regardless of Congress' eventual mix of up-front (on-budget) expenditures and off-budget bond flotation. While official Washington bones up on budget accounting trickery, CEI [Competitive Enterprise Institute] has launched its effort to shout from the rooftops that the system is broke and should be fixed.

In a September 29, 1988 Wall Street Journal [article], Fred Smith first aired his taxpayer protection plan: a cap on taxpayer liabilities. As Smith explains, taxpayer-underwritten insured accounts (accounts up to $100,000) in banks, thrifts and credit unions now total $2.7 trillion. Add to that regulators' de facto protection of all deposits in larger institutions, and taxpayers are actually held hostage to the guarantee of $4 trillion in deposits.

Under Smith's plan, George Bush would announce in 1990 a cap on federal deposit insurance. Each insured institution would receive notice that its deposit accounts, as of a certain date, were fully covered (up to $100,000). Institutions desiring to grow beyond that level would have several choices. They could: 1) purchase federal insurance from other institutions; 2) acquire private insurance; or 3) reconfigure their coverage via such options as coinsurance and deductibles.

Private insurance would thereby be phased in at the margin, likely in the form of captive insurance schemes launched by the financial institutions themselves. The private insurers at the margin could be expected to swiftly increase premiums on mismanaged and decapitalized firms, which would signal federal regulators to do the same or, at a minimum, focus their supervisory activities on these "spotlighted" institutions.

In October 1988, Smith was asked to outline his plan before a meeting of the U.S. Chamber of Commerce's Economic Policy Committee. The Committee moved to set up a task force on the thrift crisis, which continues to consult Smith as it prepares its statement on recommended reforms.

Strategically, one of CEI's key aims is to focus the collective power of various academics who have long called for a reining in of the federal safety net. CEI succeeded in bridging numerous gaps with a November 1988 letter to President-elect George Bush signed by Smith, Catherine England of the Cato Institute, Bill Haraf of the American Enterprise Institute, James Gattuso of The Heritage Foundation and Robert Litan of The Brookings Institution.

Among other things, the group recommended that Bush offer American taxpayers a package of permanent reforms including: (1) capping the total level of federal insurance; (2) insuring *depositors* rather than *deposits*; (3) setting higher capital levels for insured institutions; (4) directing that future bank/thrift failures are resolved swiftly by timely reorganization/closure; (5) developing and committing to a big bank closure/reorganization plan that does not bail out uninsured depositors and other creditors; and (6) bringing thrifts up to bank standards.

"The bankruptcy of FSLIC presents free-market champions with a unique opportunity to argue the failure of underpriced government insurance schemes."

On December 14, 1988, CEI's Jefferson Group brought together numerous Capitol Hill staffers, think tank analysts and federal regulators to examine issues of reforming federal deposit insurance. Federal Home Loan Bank Board Member Lawrence J. White argued the urgent necessity of having thrifts and banks account for their assets and liabilities in terms of current market—as opposed to book—value.

Fred Smith and others noted that while such "mark-to-market" accounting is long overdue, only partial or full privatization of deposit insurance would liberate taxpayers from regulators' inherent tendency to avoid taking action against mismanaged institutions. . . .

The Taxpayer Pays

The bankruptcy of FSLIC presents free-market champions with a unique opportunity to argue the failure of underpriced government insurance schemes and how the taxpayer, in the end, always pays. And unlike the social security debate of 1983, this time the taxpayers' role as sucker will likely figure more prominently than their role as beneficiaries of the latest failing federal insurance scheme.

Moreover, the extent to which the federal deposit insurance system is reined in will likely affect the pace at which Congress proceeds with Glass-Steagall reform. Already, some in Congress are questioning the wisdom of bank powers deregulation, fearing for the risks to which the safety net will be exposed.

Should taxpayers remain hostage to a steadily mounting guarantee of shaky financial deposit liabilities? Or should we limit taxpayer liability and put the responsibility for risk-taking back with financial institutions' managers and stockholders? To CEI, the choice is clear.

Melanie Tammen and Tom Miller direct the Competitive Enterprise Institute's financial services project. The Institute is a Washington-based pro-market public interest group.

bibliography

The following bibliography of books, periodicals,
and pamphlets is divided into chapter topics
for the reader's convenience.

The Budget Deficit

Robert L. Bartley — "Budget Deficits: A Third View," *The Wall Street Journal*, February 16, 1989.

C. Fred Bergsten — "Attacking the Deficits Now Will Bring Years of Prosperity," *Fortune*, January 2, 1989.

Alan S. Blinder — "Is the Deficit Too High? Yes. Should It Be Higher? Maybe," *Business Week*, February 20, 1989.

Ambrose Evans-Pritchard — "Voodoo Deficits," *The American Spectator*, February 1989.

Robert Heilbroner — "All Rich Nations Need Their Debt," *The Nation*, January 23, 1989.

Peter T. Kilborn — "Is the Deficit Still Dangerous? Maybe Not, Some Start To Say," *The New York Times*, January 23, 1989.

Thomas E. Mann and Charles L. Schultze — "How To End the Budget Deficit," *The World & I*, January 1989.

Charles R. Morris — "Deficit Figuring Doesn't Add Up," *The New York Times Magazine*, February 12, 1989.

Alan Murray — "The Budget Albatross," *The Wall Street Journal*, January 20, 1989.

The New Republic — "Bring Back Big Spending," March 27, 1989.

William Proxmire — "'Wizards' Say Forget the Deficit—Don't Listen," *The Wall Street Journal*, February 3, 1989.

Susan F. Rasky — "Greenspan Emphasizes Seriousness of the Budget," *The New York Times*, February 3, 1989.

Jonathan Rauch — "Is the Deficit Really So Bad?" *The Atlantic Monthly*, February 1989.

Ed Rubenstein — "No Apology Needed," *National Review*, February 10, 1989.

Rich Thomas — "Mumbo Jumbo on the Budget," *Newsweek*, February 27, 1989.

Charles Wolf Jr. — "In Hearing Deficit Alarms, We Turn a Deaf Ear to Some Positive Points," *Los Angeles Times*, February 6, 1989.

Reforming the Economy

Lindley H. Clark Jr. — "Productivity Lag May Be Management's Fault," *The Wall Street Journal*, January 11, 1989.

David P. Greanville — "The Promise of the Steady-State Economy," *The Animals' Agenda*, February 1989. Available from the Animal Rights Network, 456 Monroe Turnpike, Monroe, CT 06468.

Bennett Harrison and Barry Bluestone — *The Great U Turn*. New York: Basic Books, Inc., 1988.

Karen Elliott House — "The '90s & Beyond," *The Wall Street Journal*, January 23, 1989.

Todd May Jr. — "A Perilous Walk on the Mild Side," *Fortune*, January 16, 1989.

Ernest Morgan — "Humanizing the American Economy," *The Humanist*, November/December 1988.

Karen Pennar — "Looking Back Won't Tell You Where Prices Are Going," *Business Week*, March 13, 1989.

William H. Peterson — "Foreign Capital: Friend or Foe?" *The Freeman*, January 1989. Available from the Foundation for Economic Education, Inc., Irvington-on-the-Hudson, NY 10533.

Louis S. Richman — "When Will a Recession Hit?" *Fortune*, February 13, 1989.

Paul Craig Roberts — "It's Time To Face Facts: Supply-Side Was a Smash," *Business Week*, February 6, 1989.

Walter Shapiro — "Reaganomics with a Human Face," *Time*, February 20, 1989.

Paul L. Wachtel — "The Case Against Growth," *New Age Journal*. November/December 1988. Available from Rising Star Associates, 342 Western Ave., Brighton, MA 02135.

Paul H. Weaver — *The Suicidal Corporation: How Big Business Fails America*. New York: Simon & Schuster, 1988.

Joseph R. Wright Jr. and Beryl Sprinkel — "Reagan's Economic Critics: Wrong," *The New York Times*, January 12, 1989.

The Savings and Loan Industry

James Ring Adams — "The Big Fix," *The American Spectator*, March 1989.

Michael Allen and Andy Zipser — "As S&L Crisis Grows, FSLIC Falters in Task of Property Disposal," *The Wall Street Journal*, March 28, 1989.

Arthur F. Burns	*The Ongoing Revolution in American Banking.* Washington, DC: American Enterprise Institute, 1988.
Henry N. Butler	"Beyond the Bailout: Long-Term Solutions to the Crisis in Federal Deposit Insurance," The Heritage Foundation *Backgrounder*, March 16, 1989. Available from The Heritage Foundation, 214 Massachusetts Ave. NE, Washington, DC 20002.
Kathleen Day	"Turning Thumbs Down," *The Washington Post National Weekly Edition*, March 13/19, 1989.
Kathleen Day	"When S&Ls Handed Out More Than Just Toasters," *The Washington Post National Weekly Edition*, February 13/19, 1989.
Brad Edmondson	"The Deep, Dark Secret of Our Government," *Utne Reader*, March/April 1989.
Tom Furlong	"S&L Rescue Could Cost Average Taxpayer $450," *Los Angeles Times*, January 27, 1989.
General Accounting Office	*Troubled Financial Institutions: Solutions to the Thrift Industry Problem*, February 1989. Report available from the United States General Accounting Office, Washington, DC 20548.
Paul Getman	"The Last Temptation of Thrifts," *The Wall Street Journal*, March 23, 1989.
James K. Glassman	"Everything Must Go," *The New Republic*, October 10, 1988.
William Greider	*Secrets of the Temple.* New York: Simon & Schuster, 1988.
William Haraf and Jeremy Fand	"S&Ls—Don't Blame Deregulation," *The Washington Post National Weekly Edition*, February 6/12, 1989.
Eliot Janeway	"An Immodest Proposal for Saving the US Savings and Loan Industry," *Los Angeles Times*, December 11, 1988.
Kevin Kelly	"Taxpayers Likely To Drown in Savings and Loan Bailout," *In These Times*, March 1/14, 1989.
Martin Mayer	"Now, Woefully Fast Action on S&Ls," *The Wall Street Journal*, April 13, 1989.
Ralph Nader and Jonathan Brown	"Report to US Taxpayers on the Savings and Loan Crisis," February 1989. Available from BankWatch, PO Box 19367, Washington, DC 20036.
Nathaniel C. Nash	"In the Darwinian Age of Global Finance, Only Megabanks May Survive," *The New York Times*, June 26, 1988.
The Nation	"S&L Time Bomb," January 23, 1989.
John Paul Newport Jr.	"Why We Should Save the S&Ls," *Fortune*, April 11, 1988.
Richard W. Stevenson	"Here Are Solid Savings and Loans," *The New York Times*, February 28, 1989.
David Sylvester	"Is the Saving Rate Really That Bad?" *Fortune*, November 7, 1988.
Catherine Yang	"The 'Toxic Waste' of the Thrift Crisis," *Business Week*, March 27, 1989.

Welfare

Mimi Abramovitz	"Why Welfare Reform Is a Sham," *The Nation*, September 26, 1988.
Nancy Amidei	"What Came in Like a Lion Went out Like a Wimp," *Commonweal*, October 21, 1988.
Robert S. Bachelder	"Blinded by Metaphor: The Churches and Welfare Reform," *The Christian Century*, December 14, 1988.
Congressional Digest	"Welfare Reform," February 1988. Available from 3231 P St. NW, Washington, DC 20007.
Mary Graham	"Good Jobs at Bad Wages," *The New Republic*, November 21, 1988.
R.D. Hylton	"The New Welfare Bill: When More Isn't Enough," *Black Enterprise*, January 1989.
Nicholas Lemann	"The Unfinished War," *The Atlantic Monthly*, January 1989.
Lawrence M. Mead	"The New Welfare Debate," *Commentary*, March 1988.
Tamar A. Mehuron	"How People Get Other People Off Welfare," *Salt*, February 1989. Available from 205 W. Monroe, Chicago, IL 60606.
Richard P. Nathan	"Is the Underclass Beyond Help?" *The New York Times*, January 6, 1989.
Harrell R. Rodgers Jr., ed.	*Beyond Welfare.* Armonk, NY: M.E. Sharpe Inc., 1988.
Lisbeth B. Schorr	*Within Our Reach: Breaking the Cycle of Disadvantage.* New York: Anchor Press, 1988.
Joseph P. Shapiro	"A Conservative War on Poverty," *U.S. News & World Report*, February 27, 1989.
Daniel Wright	"Workfare: A Fine Idea in Need of Work," *Fortune*, October 24, 1988.

index

Agnos, Art, 34, 36
Aid to Families with Dependent Children
  (AFDC)
  as successful, 33
  difficult to escape, 34, 35
  effect on families, 37, 41, 42
  needs reform, 13-18, 20, 26, 27, 38-39
  see also welfare
Annunzio, Frank, 89, 91
Aponte, Robert, 37
Asians
  economic prosperity of, 49, 55
  in American society, 31, 41

Baker, Jim, 90
banking industry
  as overregulated, 85
  board of, 96, 98
    abused by S&Ls, 88-89, 90, 93
    as understaffed, 81, 95
  failures of, 51, 83, 103
  history of, 83-84
Bengal, Elsa, 34
Bernstein, Peter L., 9
blacks
  and poverty, 36, 48
  and welfare, 14, 36
    as beneficial, 37-39
    as harmful, 41-43
Bowman, Robert, 64-65
Brady, Nicholas F., 97, 101
Broder, David S., 64
Brookes, Warren T., 45
budget deficit
  and S&L crisis, 94
  causes of
    excessive government spending, 3-4, 6,
      72, 77
      on defense, 63, 66
        con, 67, 77
    high interest rates, 6-7, 51
    lack of economic growth, 51
  legislation to curtail
    Deficit Reduction Act, 27
    Gramm-Rudman-Hollings, 4
  threatens the economy, 1-2, 5-7, 63, 76
    con, 9-12, 70, 72
  ways to reduce
    budget cuts, 2, 4
      in the military, 63, 65, 66
      may be impossible, 4
    economic growth, 1, 2, 72, 77
      con, 3-4, 7
    government deregulation, 73
      con, 77, 78
    increased taxes, 1, 3, 18
      dangers of, 11, 69
    individual savings, 2, 3, 6
      con, 11

welfare cuts, 18, 27
Bush, George, 9, 52, 77, 79, 88, 90
  plan to save S&Ls, 91, 93, 94, 97-99
    will fail, 101-103

Carter administration, 47, 76, 77, 78
Carter, Hodding, 67, 68
Castellblanch, Ramon, 59
child care
  and child support payments, 14-16,
    38-39
  government assistance
    as needed, 13, 16, 29, 34, 36
      con, 30-31
  helps children, 20-21
  need for, 20-21, 28, 33-34, 35, 38
    as exaggerated, 29
Cohen, Stephen, 60-61
Competitive Enterprise Institute (CEI), 102,
  103
Congress
  and the deficit, 4, 5, 63
  and S&Ls
    corruption in, 87, 95, 102
    deregulation of, 79, 80, 81, 95, 97
    and tax bills, 71
    and welfare reform, 23, 24, 27
Cranston, Alan, 87, 91

Darman, Richard, 94
Dash, Leon, 42
Day, Kathleen, 87
day care. *See* child care
debt
  international, 9-10
  national, 45, 51, 70
  see also budget deficit
defense spending
  harms economy, 63-66
    con, 67-70, 77
Deukmejian, George, 27, 36
Drucker, Peter, 46
Dukakis, Michael, 17, 18, 27

economic theories
  Keynesian, 3, 10-11
  monetarism, 52
  Reaganomics
    as successful, 71-73
      con, 75-78
  supply-side, 3, 10-11, 41, 52
economy
  European, 46, 47, 57, 68, 69, 71, 72
  global
    as slowing, 51, 66, 68
      con, 55, 75
  US
    and foreign nations
      as dependent on, 53, 66

comparisons with
  Great Britain, 7, 9-11, 25, 46, 48,
    71, 75
  Japan, 5, 9-11, 45, 47, 48, 49, 50,
    51, 52, 56, 57, 58, 64, 68, 69, 71,
    72
  must reclaim markets in, 55, 57
  as strong, 45-48, 71-73
    con, 5-7, 49-53, 75-78
  dollar's role in, 55, 57, 58, 60
  growth of, 45-46, 48, 57
    problems hindering, 50
      deficit as, 1-2, 4
      military spending as, 63-66
        con, 67-70
    will help poor, 38, 39, 47-48
  industry's role in
    as declining, 59-62
    as strong, 55-58, 73
  Third World's effect on, 51, 52, 72
education, 34, 35, 38
Eisenhower, Dwight D., 68
Ellwood, David, 13, 14, 16, 17, 18
England, Catherine, 83, 103

families
  black
    aided by welfare, 37-39
      con, 36, 41-43
    headed by women, 13, 14, 15, 20, 24,
      29, 36, 37-38, 39, 41
    threaten society, 41
Family Security Act
  description of, 13-18
  will be helpful, 19-21
    con, 23-24
FDIC (Federal Deposit Insurance
  Corporation), 90-91, 93, 94-99
Financial Forecaster, 49
Forbes, Malcolm S. Jr., 71
Fuller, Craig, 88

Garn, Jake, 88, 90, 91
Garn-St. Germain Act, 79, 88, 89, 90
Gilder, Alan, 72-73
Goldwater, Barry, 64
Gonzalez, Henry, 79, 94
Gould, George, 90
Gramm-Rudman-Hollings law, 4
Gray, Edwin, 80, 81, 88-90, 95-96
Greenspan, Alan, 5-7, 94
Gross National Product (GNP)
  and budget deficit, 1, 2-3, 4, 5, 7, 77
  and foreign savings, 7
  as growing, 45, 46, 48, 68, 78
    myth of, 49
  manufacturing's share of, 61
    as shrinking, 59, 60
  military's share of, 64, 79-80

Hacker, Andrew, 13
Hamilton, Lee H., 64
Hohlt, Richard, 88, 90
Homestead program, 42-43

industry
  as healthy, 55-58
    con, 59-62
inflation
  and interest rates, 6
  as decreasing, 49
  causes of
    budget deficit, 1
      con, 9, 10
    trade deficit, 58
  effects of, 52, 81
interest rates
  as causing deficit, 6, 7
    con, 10-11
  as harming economy, 51, 66
  in S&L industry, 79, 87-88, 89, 95
investment
  as increasing, 69, 71, 72-73
    con, 78
  foreign, 46, 49, 50, 51
  in S&Ls, 80, 98
    as uncontrolled, 81, 89, 95
  role in economy
    as shifting, 56, 66
    during deficit, 6-7

Jacobs, Irwin, 47
Japan
  economy of, 9-11, 47, 48, 49
    and trade, 72
  savings rate in, 5
  taxes in, 71
  US relations with, 45, 51, 52, 56, 57, 64,
    68
job training programs
  are effective, 35
  are necessary, 38
  are politicized, 34, 36
  in California (GAIN), 26, 33, 34-35, 36
  in Massachusetts (ET), 17, 18, 26, 35
    Denise Richards case, 33-34, 36
  in Minnesota, 26, 35
  JOBS (Job Opportunities and Basic Skills
    Training Program), 19, 20, 21
  Jobs Training Partnership Act, 28
    problems of, 16-17, 23-24, 25, 26, 29,
      30-31, 34, 35
    stigmatizes participants, 36
  Work Incentive Program (WIN), 27-28

Kelly, Kevin, 79
Kuttner, Robert, 79

labor
  and workfare, 21, 26
  productivity, 46, 47, 50, 77
    as hindered by deficit, 2, 6
  wages, 57, 60, 61, 65
Leach, Jim, 93, 96

McGee, Carolyn, 35
Mead, Lawrence M., 29
Medicaid, 23-24, 26, 76
men
  and child support, 14, 15-16, 18, 20
  as absent fathers, 14, 15, 20, 29, 36

black, 36, 37
Miller, John, 59
Miller, Tom, 101
mortgages, 6
  from S&Ls, 79, 81, 85, 97
    are no longer needed, 80, 91, 96
Moynihan, Daniel Patrick, 13, 15, 17, 19,
  20, 21, 38, 39
Murray, Charles, 23, 35, 73

Nasar, Sylvia, 55
Neckerman, Kathryn, 37
New Republic, The, 19
Nixon, Richard, 29

O'Connell, William, 88, 89, 90
Omnibus Budget Reconciliation Act
  (OBRA), 27
O'Sullivan, John L., 63

Penner, Rudolph, 10-11
poverty, 32
  blacks in
    are helped by welfare, 37-39
      con, 41-43
  children in, 20, 41
    are ignored, 36
    programs for, 16, 39
  women in, 13-14, 20, 23-24, 41
Pratt, Richard, 88, 90

Reagan administration
  and the economy, 4, 45, 46, 47, 51, 52,
    60, 71, 75, 76, 77, 78
  and military spending, 63, 64, 65, 68
  and poverty, 26, 33, 66
  and S&Ls, 80, 81, 88, 89, 90, 91
Reaganomics
  as a success, 71-73
    con, 75-78
Regan, Donald, 89-90
Reynolds, Alan, 72-73
Riegle, Donald, 87, 91, 93
Rockefeller, John D., 65
Rothschild, Emma, 75
Rudolph, Barbara, 93

St. Germain, Fernand J., 87, 88, 91
savings & loans (S&Ls)
  are unstable, 80, 81, 84
  crisis in, 93-96
    causes of
      corruption, 87-91, 95, 96
      deregulation, 79-81, 95
      regulation, 83-86
    government should save, 97-99
      con, 81, 84, 101-103
    history of, 79, 81, 87-88
savings rate
  as low, 5, 76
    con, 46
  can cushion economy, 1, 7
  deficit destroys, 5, 6
    con, 11
Sawhill, Isabel, 13, 14, 16, 17, 35
Scowcroft, Brent, 65
Smith, Fred, 102-103
Social Security, 11, 16, 76
Soviet Union, 67, 68
Stein, Herbert, 1, 67

Taggart, Larry, 90
Tammen, Melanie, 101
taxes, 71, 76
  as necessary to save S&Ls, 79, 80, 81,
    90-91, 93
  Bush plan, 94, 95, 97-99
  unfairness of, 102, 103
  deductions, 39, 41
  reform, 4, 71
teenage mothers, 42, 73
  need welfare, 35-36
    con, 17, 18, 38, 39, 41
  should stay in school, 31
Thornburgh, Richard, 95
thrifts. See savings & loans
Thurow, Lester, 49, 66
trade deficit, 1, 5, 11, 60
  and exports, 55, 56, 57
  and surpluses, 59, 72
  as exaggerated, 45, 46-47, 58
  causes of, 56
    deindustrialization, 61
    military spending, 63-66
  harms US, 51
    con, 11, 72
Tucker, William, 41

unemployment, 17
  among blacks, 36, 37-39
  rates, 49, 50
US League of Savings Institutions, 88, 89, 90,
  91

Vartanian, Thomas, 88

Wall, M. Danny, 80, 88, 90-91, 96
Walsh, Joan, 33
Washington Spectator, The, 63
welfare
  and job programs, 13, 17, 18, 19, 25-28
    should be required, 16, 20, 29-32
      con, 33-36
    training provided by, 16-17, 27-28, 29,
      30-31, 32
  and women, 13-14, 15, 16, 17
    encourages teenage motherhood, 17,
      18, 41, 42-43
    harms, 23-24
  helps black families, 37-39
    con, 36, 41-43
  promotes dependency, 13, 15, 17, 18,
    24, 26-29, 31-32, 39, 42-43, 76
  reform, 26, 27
    description of, 13-18
      Homestead program, 42-43
    will be beneficial, 19-21
      con, 23-24
Weyrich, Paul, 43
Wilson, William Julius, 36, 37
Wiseman, Michael, 25
women
  and child support, 14, 16
  and job training, 16, 27, 33
  black, 41
  need child care, 16, 20, 29, 34, 36
  on welfare, 13-14, 15, 16, 17, 18, 23-24,
    29
Wright, Jim, 80, 87, 90, 91

Zysman, John, 60-61